I CAN'T BELIEVE I'M
Loom Knitting!

Have you discovered the hot new tool that makes knitting easier than ever before? It's a knitting loom! And the creative options are so exciting!

Knitting looms (a.k.a. "knitting wheels") come in several shapes and sizes. Using a loom is as simple as wrapping yarn around the pegs and lifting the yarn loops with a tool. And there are a huge variety of beautiful stitch patterns to create with looms!

Our clear photos and instructions make it a breeze to knit three hats with fun loom techniques. In addition, the Sampler Afghan uses a different pattern stitch for each of its 12 squares—the same pattern stitches used for the rest of the 14 projects, which include scarves, a tote, gloves, a wrap, and a vest.

Before you know it, you'll find yourself saying, "I can't believe I'm loom knitting!"

LEISURE ARTS, INC.
Little Rock, Arkansas

table of CONTENTS

TOOLS

Knitting looms are called by many names. And you'll be surprised at how versatile they are, no matter their shape.

Round Loom—also known as a "round wheel, knitting wheel, spool, or reel." It can be made of nylon, wood, or plastic. Round looms come in many sizes, and the five that we used for our projects had 24, 31, 36, 41, and 48 pegs. With round looms, you can make a tubular shape that works great for a hat or a flat shape that's perfect for a scarf.

Straight Loom—also known as "straight wheel, rectangle loom, a knitting board, and infinity rake"—can be made out of nylon or wood. Straight looms come in different lengths ranging from 9½" to 60" (24 cm to 152.5 cm). They can be used for a variety of projects. We used three sizes that have a peg on each end in addition to the usual side pegs. These looms had 38, 50, and 62 pegs, allowing us to make large flat items such as a tote, pillow, shawl, vest, and even a baby blanket. Straight looms can also be used for circular knitting to make hats and gloves.

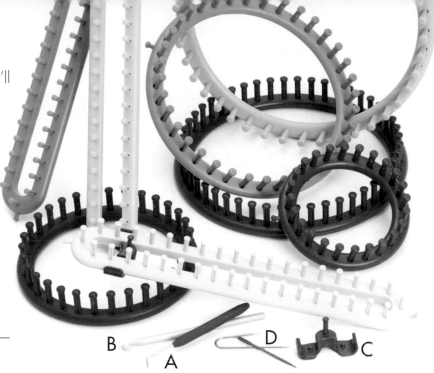

B · A · D · C

A. Knitting loom tool—A special tool to help you lift the bottom loop on each peg over the top loop or working yarn. Some looms come with the tool or it can be purchased separately. A yarn needle, knitting needle, or even a nut pick can be substituted for the tool.

B. Crochet hook—Some of the projects require a crochet hook to work the cast on or bind off row. A hook is also used to attach an I-Cord Edging to an afghan. Use size K (6.5 mm) or any size large enough to catch the strand(s) of yarn.

C. Loom clip—A loom clip is a plastic bridge that clips onto the bottom of a straight loom. It provides an extra peg in the center of the loom so that small tubes can be made, such as fingers for gloves.

D. Cable needle—When making cables, stitches are removed from the pegs and placed on a cable needle while other stitches are being worked. We used a U-shaped cable needle.

GETTING STARTED

The best way to learn how to knit on the knitting loom is to jump right in and make a hat. By following the steps on pages 4-7, you will make your first hat while learning the basics. You can continue gaining more experience and learning additional techniques while you make two more hats by following the steps on pages 8-13. Your hats can be any size; the yarn, the size of the loom, and how loose or tight you form the stitches determines the finished size. Use the hat sizing information below as a guide when choosing a loom for the three beginner hats. As you become more at ease with the techniques, you should be able to achieve the gauge called for in each project (see Gauge, page 26), so that your projects will be the proper size.

HAT SIZING

Pegs	Size	Head Circumference	
24	preemie	9-14"	(23-35.5 cm)
31	infant	14-18"	(35.5-45.5 cm)
36	child	18-20"	(45.5-51 cm)
41	adult	20-24"	(51-61 cm)

circular loom knitting BASICS

The term "circular" refers to working in the round, not the shape of the loom. You will learn how to knit flat pieces on the Round loom beginning on page 14.

BEGINNER KNIT HAT

You will need the following materials:

Medium Weight Yarn [1.76 ounces, 87 yards (50 grams, 80 meters) per skein]: 1 skein

Round loom - any size (see hat sizing on page 3)

Knitting loom tool

Yarn needle

HAT INSTRUCTIONS

Follow E-Wrap Cast On to begin.

E-WRAP CAST ON ....

The initial wrap of the loom is called the **cast on row**. It is the simplest cast on method for loom knitting.

Make a slip knot (**Figs. 17a-c, page 27**), leaving a 6" (15 cm) end. Insert the slip knot into the center of the loom from top to bottom and place it on the side peg, pulling the strand to tighten the loop (**Fig. 1a**). This **anchors the yarn end** and will hold the beginning of your cast on in place. Once the anchored yarn is removed, the yarn end will hang to the inside of the loom.

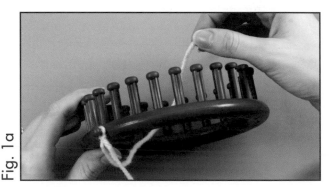

Fig. 1a

TIP
It is absolutely essential to wrap the working yarn loose enough to be able to later lift the loop off the peg, but not so loose that it falls off. As you wrap, let the yarn gently slide through your hand.

PLEASE NOTE

The color or shape of the loom (straight or round), the color of the yarn, or the number of strands used for the Figs. will not necessarily match all of the projects, but the techniques illustrated will be the same. They are for reference purposes only.

Holding the loom however it is most comfortable to you, wrap the working yarn around the first peg (peg A) in a clockwise direction, ending at the inside of the loom and behind the next peg (*Fig. 1b*).

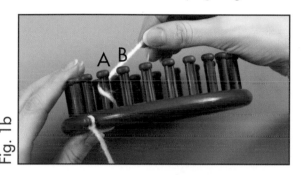

Fig. 1b

Moving around the loom counter-clockwise and wrapping each peg with the same tension, wrap the next peg (peg B) clockwise, ending at the inside of the loom and behind the next peg (*Fig. 1c*).

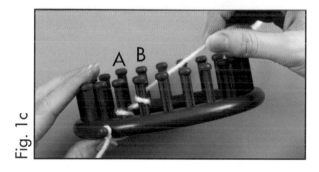

Fig. 1c

Continue around the loom, pushing the loops down with your other hand as you go, until all of the pegs have been wrapped, ending at the inside of the loom (*Fig. 1d*).

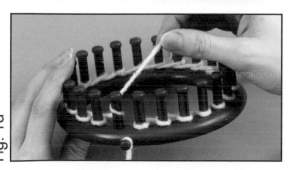

Fig. 1d

TIP

As you push the loops down, leave your finger on the last loop to prevent it from falling off.

The yarn should cross at the inside edge of each peg on the loom (*Fig. 1e*), while leaving a loop on the outside of each peg (*Fig. 1f*).

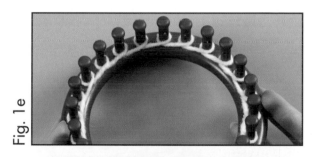

Fig. 1e

Fig. 1f

Beginner Knit Hat
After all of the pegs have been wrapped, follow Knit Stitch on page 6 to work the body of your hat.

KNIT STITCH
(abbreviated K)

Step 1: Working in the same direction as the cast on, loosely lay the working yarn on the outside of the loom, **above** the loops on the pegs *(Fig. 2a)*.

Fig. 2a

Step 2: Using the tool, lift the bottom loop over the working yarn and off the peg *(Fig. 2b)*, allowing a new stitch to form around the peg *(Fig. 2c)*. Push the new loop down with your other hand.

Fig. 2b

Fig. 2c

Repeat Steps 1 and 2 for each peg to be knitted.

TIP The working yarn should wrap around the peg as it forms a stitch. The stitches will form naturally if you gently push the back of the previous stitches down as you work.

After working 2 or 3 rounds, remove the anchored yarn from the side peg and allow the bottom of the piece to hang free.

TIP To prevent loops from accidently falling off the pegs, remember to push them down as you create them. If the bottom loop is too tight, it will be more likely to push the working yarn off the peg as you lift it over. If this happens, place the loop back onto the peg. Loosen your tension as you form the stitches.

The spacing of the pegs stretches the width of the stitches *(Fig. 2d)*. Before measuring the length of the knitted piece, give a tug holding the cast on edge and the loom to pull the stitches until they look evenly worked *(Fig. 2e)*.

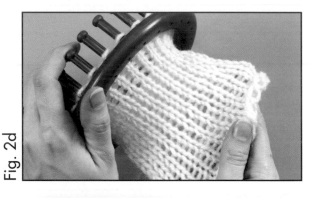

Fig. 2d

Fig. 2e

····························

The right side of the piece hangs towards the outside of the loom (**Fig. 2f**), and the wrong side to the inside (**Fig. 2g**). Knitting every round forms Stockinette Stitch.

This technique is used to take circularly knitted projects off the loom by gathering the stitches together, and is perfect for closing the top of a hat or the toe on a stocking.

right side

Fig. 2f

Thread a yarn needle with the yarn end. Beginning with the last peg worked, insert the yarn needle in the loop from bottom to top (**Fig. 3a**) and lift it off the peg, sliding it onto the yarn end. Repeat for each loop around the loom.

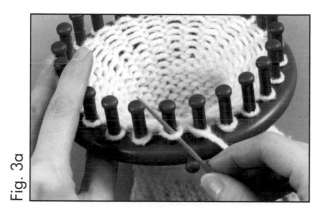

Fig. 3a

wrong side

Fig. 2g

With the yarn end to the **wrong** side of the project, pull the end tightly, gathering the loops to the center (**Fig. 3b**); knot the yarn tightly and weave in the end; clip end close to work.
Weave in beginning yarn end.

Beginner Knit Hat

Continue to knit every peg for each round for the following finished length, allowing the bottom edge to roll:

Preemie size: 5½" to 6½" (14 cm to 16.5 cm)
Infant size: 6½" to 7½" (16.5 cm to 19 cm)
Child size: 7½" to 8½" (19 cm to 21.5 cm)
Adult size: 8½" to 9" (21.5 cm to 23 cm)

Cut yarn leaving an 18" (45.5 cm) length for sewing.

Follow Gather Removal to complete your hat.

Fig. 3b

Congratulations! You finished your first project and you have learned the e-wrap cast on, the knit stitch, and the gathered removal and you have a great hat to show for it.
Now move on to the Next-step E-wrap hat on page 8 to learn more.

NEXT-STEP E-WRAP KNIT HAT

This hat will teach you how to work the E-wrap Knit Stitch circularly.

You will need the following materials:
Medium Weight Yarn [1.76 ounces, 87 yards (50 grams, 80 meters) per skein]:
   Preemie and infant sizes - 1 skein
   Child and adult sizes - 2 skeins
Round loom - any size (see hat sizing on page 3)
Knitting loom tool
Yarn needle

HAT INSTRUCTIONS

Holding 2 strands of yarn together and treating them as one throughout knitting your hat, E-Wrap Cast On (*Figs. 1a-f, pages 4 and 5*) onto all pegs.

Follow E-Wrap Knit Stitch to work the body of your hat.

E-WRAP KNIT STITCH ....
(abbreviated EWK)

The first step of this stitch is worked like the E-Wrap Cast On. (Holding 2 strands of yarn together makes a thick, warm fabric.)

Step 1 (Wrapping row): Continue around the loom in the same direction as the cast on, wrapping the pegs clockwise a second time until all of the pegs have 2 loops on them, again pushing the loops down as you go and ending at the inside of the loom (*Fig. 4a*).

Fig. 4a

Step 2 (Completing e-wrap knit stitches): Drop the working yarn. Using the tool, lift the bottom loop on the **last** peg wrapped over the top loop and off the peg (*Fig. 4b*). This completes the e-wrap knit stitch and secures the working yarn. Working in either direction, continue around lifting the bottom loop over the top loop and off the peg, also pushing the new loops down with your other hand as you go until there is one loop remaining on each peg.

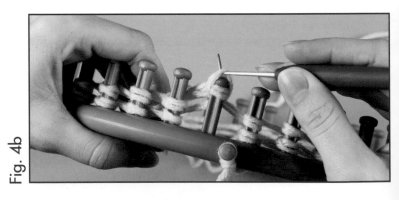

Fig. 4b

For each of the following rounds, wrap each peg clockwise, ending at the inside of the loom (2 loops on each peg). Then, complete the e-wrap knit stitches (step 2).

After working 2 or 3 rounds, remove the anchored yarn from the side peg and allow the bottom of the piece to hang free.

The right side of the piece hangs towards the outside of the loom (*Fig. 4c*), and the wrong side to the inside (*Fig. 4d*). The yarn at the base of each stitch is crossed and forms what is known as a twisted stitch. E-wrap knitting every round forms Twisted Stockinette Stitch.

right side

Fig. 4c

wrong side

Fig. 4d

Next-Step E-Wrap Knit Hat

Continue to e-wrap knit every peg for each round for the following finished length, allowing the bottom edge to roll:
Preemie size: 5½" to 6½" (14 cm to 16.5 cm)
Infant size: 6½" to 7½" (16.5 cm to 19 cm)
Child size: 7½" to 8½" (19 cm to 21.5 cm)
Adult size: 8½" to 9" (21.5 cm to 23 cm)

Cut yarn leaving an 18" (45.5cm) length for sewing.

Work Gathered Removal to remove your hat from the loom and to close the top (*Figs. 3a & b, page 7*).

Congratulations! You finished your second project and you have learned the e-wrap knit stitch and you have another great hat to show for it.
Now move on to the Garter Stitch Brim hat on page 10 to learn more.

GARTER STITCH BRIM HAT

You will begin your hat by learning the Chain Cast On, then learn the Purl Stitch (page 12) and how to alternate a round of purl stitches with a round of knit stitches (page 6). You will see how easy it is to use multiple colors in your projects.

You will need the following materials:
Medium Weight Yarn [1.76 ounces, 87 yards (50 grams, 80 meters) per skein]:
   Color A (Teal) - 1 skein
   Color B (Gold) - 1 skein
Round loom - any size (see hat sizing on page 3)
Knitting loom tool
Crochet hook, size K (6.5 mm)
Yarn needle

CHAIN CAST ON ....

The chain cast on method produces a tighter cast on and gives your projects a more finished edge than the e-wrap cast on.

Leaving a 6" (15 cm) end, place a slip knot on the crochet hook (*Figs. 17a-c, page 27*).

You will cast on **counter-clockwise** working on the inside of the loom. Hold the crochet hook inside the loom. Wrap the working yarn around the outside of the first peg and bring it to the inside (*Fig. 5a*).

Fig. 5a

Lay the working yarn on top of the crochet hook with the peg being encircled by the yarn. Catching the working yarn with the hook (*Fig. 5b*), bring it through the loop on the hook, producing a chain stitch with the peg in the middle of the chain stitch.

Fig. 5b

HAT INSTRUCTIONS
Using Color A, follow Chain Cast On for all pegs.

Pull the loop on the hook large enough to reach the next peg in order to easily cast on the next stitch (*Fig. 5c*).

Fig. 5c

★ For the next cast on stitch, wrap the working yarn around the outside of the next peg and bring it to the inside, lay the working yarn on top of the crochet hook, catch the yarn and bring it through the loop on the hook.

Repeat from ★ until you have cast on all but one peg.

For the last cast on stitch, keep the working yarn to the inside of the loom and place the loop from the hook onto the last empty peg (*Fig. 5d*).

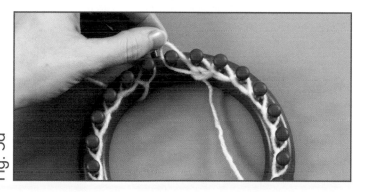

Fig. 5d

Note: When making a project that you are instructed to chain cast on **clockwise**, you will need to hold the loom with the outer edge facing you and the working yarn and crochet hook inside the loom. Work the same as before, wrapping the yarn around the outside of the pegs (*Fig. 5e*).

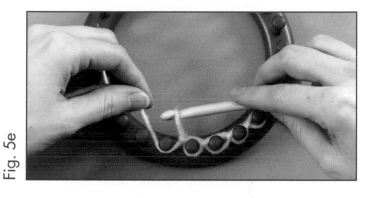

Fig. 5e

Garter Stitch Brim Hat
After all of the pegs have been cast on, work Round 1 in the purl stitch, page 12.

PURL STITCH
(abbreviated P)

Step 1: Lay the working yarn on the outside of the loom, **below** the loops on the pegs (*Fig. 6a*).

Fig. 6a

Step 2: Insert the tool down through the loop on the peg (from top to bottom) (*Fig. 6b*).

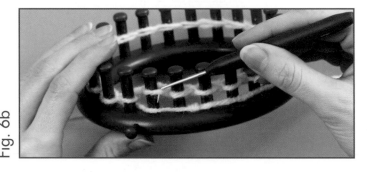

Fig. 6b

Step 3: With the tip of the tool over the working yarn, turn the tool as you pull the working yarn up through the loop on the peg forming a new loop (*Fig. 6c*).

Fig. 6c

Step 4: Using your fingers, lift the original loop off the peg. Place the newly formed loop onto the empty peg (*Fig. 6d*). Tighten the loop by gently pulling the working yarn, allowing the stitch to curve around the outside half of the peg.

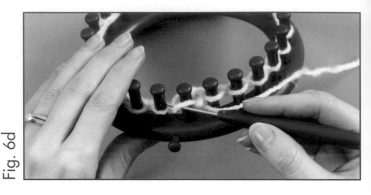

Fig. 6d

Repeat Steps 1-4 for each peg to be purled.

Garter Stitch Brim Hat
Round 2: Knit around (*Figs. 2 a-c, page 6*).
Round 3: Purl around.
Repeat Rounds 2 and 3, forming Garter Stitch, for the following length, ending by working a **purl** round:
Infant and Preemie size: 1½" (4 cm)
Child size: 2" (5 cm)
Adult size: 2½" (6.5 cm)

Body
The body is worked only using the knit stitch, changing colors every 4 rounds to form stripes.
To add stripes to your hat, follow Changing Colors Rounds 1-12, page 13, then repeat Rounds 5-12 once for Preemie size, twice for Child and Infant sizes, and 3 times for adult size.

Cut Color A. Cut Color B leaving an 18" (45.5 cm) length for sewing.
Work Gathered Removal to remove your hat from the loom and to close the top (*Figs. 3a & b, page 7*).

Congratulations! Now you can chain cast on, purl, and change colors. There are more exciting techniques waiting for you beginning on page 14.

CHANGING COLORS ···

CIRCULAR KNITTING

To change colors on the next round, and then every 4 rounds, work as follows:

Round 1: Drop the color you are using to the inside of the loom (Color A). Place the beginning yarn end of the next color (Color B) at the inside of the loom *(Fig. 7a)* and knit around.

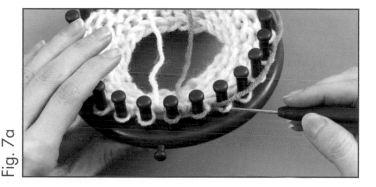

Fig. 7a

Round 2: Knit around.
Round 3: Twist Colors A and B to prevent long strands across the back of each stripe *(Fig. 7b)*, then continuing with Color B, knit around.

Fig. 7b

Round 4: Knit around.
Round 5: Drop Color B to the inside of the loom, then pick up Color A from underneath the strand *(Fig. 7c)* and knit around.

Fig. 7c

Round 6: Knit around.
Round 7: Twist Colors A and B, then continuing with Color A, knit around.
Round 8: Knit around.
Round 9: Drop Color A to the inside of the loom, then pick up Color B and knit around.
Round 10: Knit around.
Round 11: Twist Colors A and B, then continuing with Color B, knit around.
Round 12: Knit around.

FLAT KNITTING

The first time the second color is used, make a slip knot and attach it to the side peg *(Fig. 1a, page 4)*. Work the stripe as indicated in the individual instructions.

When changing to the next color, drop the color that you are working with to the inside of the loom. Then pick up the next color from underneath the strand *(Fig. 7d)*. This will create a neat edge along your knitting.

Fig. 7d

When changing colors every four rows, twist the yarns before working the third row of each stripe *(Fig. 7e)*. This will prevent long strands along the edge.

Fig. 7e

flat loom knitting **BASICS**

To create a flat piece, work back and forth in rows, either on the round loom or on the straight loom.

Cast on the number of pegs according to the instructions.

TIP When chain casting on *(page 10)*, cast on one peg less than needed. Keep the working yarn to the inside and place the loop from the hook onto the last peg needed.

The knit stitch *(page 6)* and the purl stitch *(page 12)* are worked the same for flat loom knitting as they are for circular loom knitting, no matter which direction you are working.

The Sampler Afghan on page 28 is perfect for learning the techniques on pages 14-23.

Let's make a practice swatch of flat loom knitting.

E-WRAP KNIT STITCH ·······
(abbreviated EWK)

Unlike circular knitting where the pegs are always e-wrapped clockwise, in flat knitting the direction of the e-wrap depends on the direction that the row will be worked.

To practice the E-Wrap Knit Stitch, begin by working the E-Wrap Cast On *(page 4)* onto 5 pegs of any loom, holding 2 strands of yarn together and treating them as one throughout.

THE FIRST RIGHT TO LEFT ROW
Step 1: Wrap the last peg worked clockwise *(Fig. 8a)*.

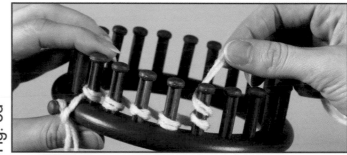
Fig. 8a

Step 2: Working to your left, wrap each remaining peg **counter-clockwise** until all of the pegs have 2 loops on them *(Fig. 8b)*.

Fig. 8b

Step 3: Using the tool and beginning with the last peg wrapped *(Fig. 8c)*, lift the bottom loop on each peg over the top loop and off the peg, completing the e-wrap knit stitches *(Fig. 8d)*.

Fig. 8c

Fig. 8d

LEFT TO RIGHT ROW
Step 4 (Wrapping row): Wrap the first peg counter-clockwise *(Fig. 8e)*, then working to your right, wrap each remaining peg clockwise *(Fig. 8f)*.

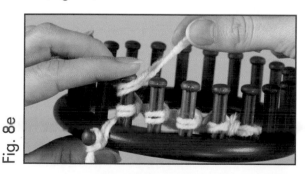

Fig. 8e

Fig. 8f

Step 5 (Completing e-wrap knit stitches): Using the tool and beginning with the last peg wrapped, lift the bottom loop on each peg over the top loop and off the peg.

RIGHT TO LEFT ROW
Step 6 (Wrapping row): Wrap the first peg clockwise, then working to your left, wrap each remaining peg **counter-clockwise**.

Step 7 (Completing e-wrap knit stitches): Using the tool and beginning with the last peg wrapped, lift the bottom loop on each peg over the top loop and off the peg.

TIP

There is an easy way to remember which direction to wrap the pegs for each row. The first peg is wrapped in the **same** direction as the last stitch on the previous row. The remaining pegs are wrapped in the **opposite** direction as the first peg.

Repeat Steps 4-7, ending by working Step 5 or 7.

After working 2 or 3 rows, remove the anchored yarn from the side peg and allow the bottom of the piece to hang free.

To remove your practice swatch from the loom, follow Chain One Bind Off on page 16.

additional **TECHNIQUES**

CHAIN ONE BIND OFF ·············

Binding off is a process that removes the loops from the pegs of the loom and secures the stitches.

With the working yarn to the inside of the loom, insert a crochet hook in the loop on the last peg worked, from bottom to top, and lift it off the peg. To chain 1, lay the working yarn on top of the crochet hook and bring it through the loop on the hook (**Fig. 9 a**), insert the hook in the loop on the next peg, lift it off the peg and pull it through the loop on the hook (**Fig. 9b**), ★ chain 1, insert the hook in the loop on the next peg, lift it off the peg and pull it through the loop on the hook.

Fig. 9a

Fig. 9b

Fig. 9c

When binding off all stitches, repeat from ★ until all of the loops have been removed from the loom and there is one loop left on the crochet hook. Chain 1, cut the yarn and pull the end through the final loop (**Fig. 9c**); tighten the loop.

When binding off a certain number of stitches for an Armhole or other shaping, repeat from ★ for each additional peg to be bound off. Bind off one extra peg and place the loop from the crochet hook back onto the empty peg. Count the pegs remaining to be sure you have the correct amount.

Note: If the last row was worked from right to left, you will need to hold the loom with the inner edge facing while binding off.

SKIPPING PEGS ·

Skipping pegs gives the same result as slipping stitches in hand knitting. This techique is used for several reasons—one is to create colored and textured patterns while another is to create a more finished look to the vertical edge of flat panels. To use this technique, simply don't wrap or knit the peg to be skipped. It is referred to as skip 1 (or skip 2). The working yarn can be placed on the wrong side or the right side of the work, depending on the desired result.

Most often, the working yarn is placed on the wrong side, at the inside of the loom and across the skipped peg(s), allowing you to work a row with one color, and achieve the effect of alternating two colors. Many color patterns can be formed such as an overall color design, vertical stripes, diagonal stripes, and the illusion of a color in front of a second color.

Simulated Basketweave, page 33

Corn on the Cob, page 31

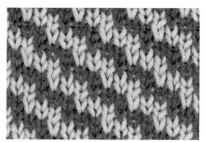

Diagonal Stripe, page 32

Two-Toned Lattice, page 32

When instructed to **skip a peg**, bring the working yarn to the inside of the loom, across the peg to be skipped and ready to e-wrap knit the next peg **or** back to the outside, ready to knit or purl the next peg (*Fig. 10a*). The strand will **not** show on the right side.

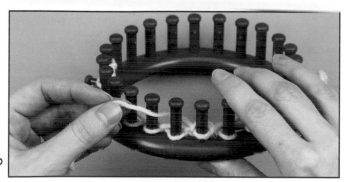

Fig. 10a

The second method which places the working yarn in **front** of the worked piece, forms a horizontal strand on the right side for an interesting texture. The yarn will need to be placed behind the pegs and still be in front of the work.

Honeycomb, page 31

When instructed to **skip a peg with yarn in front** (*abbreviated skip 1 WYIF*), use the tool to lift the loop from the peg to be skipped and hold it on the tool. Bring the yarn in front of the loop on the tool and behind the empty peg, then to the outside of the loom (*Fig. 10b*) Put the loop on the tool back onto the peg. The strand will show on the right side.

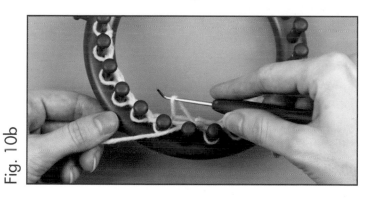

Fig. 10b

CABLES ······································

Cables are used in the Sampler Afghan, page 28, and also in Robin's Hood, page 54.

There are many variations of cable patterns, but all are based on switching the position of stitches on the pegs. The Left Cross and Right Cross cables are made up of 4 knit stitches surrounded by 2 purl stitches on each side, so that the cables rise above the fabric. A **cable needle** is used to hold 2 of the stitches in the cable while the other 2 stitches are moved to the newly vacated pegs.

The direction in which the top stitches lean is dependent on which group of stitches are placed on the cable needle—the first group or second group. These cables are worked on a **right** to **left** row.

To learn how to make cables, you can make the following sample. Cables use knit stitches *(page 6)* and purl stitches *(page 12)*.

Using any round loom, chain cast on 8 pegs **clockwise** *(Fig. 5e, page 11)*.
Rows 1-3: Purl 2 pegs, knit 4 pegs, purl 2 pegs.
Row 4: Purl 2 pegs, work either Left Cross Cable *(see below)* or Right Cross Cable *(page 19)*, purl 2 pegs.
Repeat Rows 1-4 until you are comfortable making cables.

LEFT CROSS CABLE (uses next 4 pegs)
Bring the working yarn to the inside of the loom, across the next 2 pegs (pegs A & B), then back to the outside *(Fig. 11a)* and **loosely** knit the next 2 pegs (pegs C & D), then place them onto a cable needle *(Fig. 11b)* and let it hang at the inside of the loom.

Left Cross Cable

Right Cross Cable

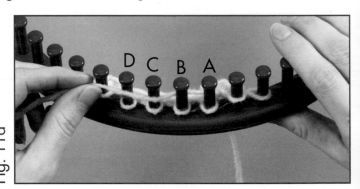

Fig. 11a

Fig. 11b

Bring the working yarn to the inside of the loom, and across all 4 pegs (pegs A-D), then to the outside before the first skipped peg (peg A) *(Fig. 11c)*. Knit the 2 skipped pegs, then use the tool to move them to the empty pegs, keeping them in the same order *(Fig. 11d)*. Place the stitches from the cable needle onto the newly vacated pegs, keeping them in the same order *(Fig. 11e)*. Tighten the stitches to prevent elongated stitches.

TIP

The stitches should always be worked **loosely**, allowing them to be easily moved. If the stitches are tight, try knitting them by wrapping the yarn twice around the pegs, then lift the bottom loop over both loops. Once the cable stitches have been moved, take up the slack of each stitch by gently tugging on the yarn.

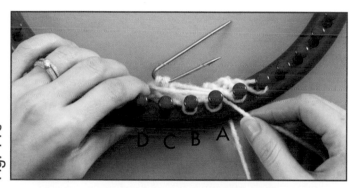

Fig. 11c

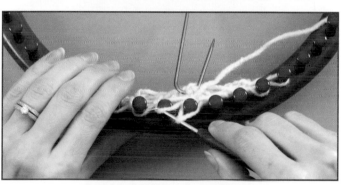

Fig. 11d

Fig. 11e

RIGHT CROSS CABLE (uses next 4 pegs)

Place the stitches from the next 2 pegs (pegs A & B) onto a cable needle and let it hang at the inside of the loom. Bring the working yarn behind the 2 empty pegs and to the outside of the loom *(Fig. 11f)*.

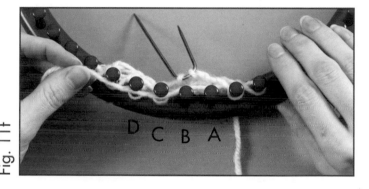

Fig. 11f

Knit the next 2 pegs (pegs C & D), then use the tool to move them to the empty pegs, keeping them in the same order *(Fig. 11g)*. With the working yarn outside the loom, place the stitches from the cable needle onto the newly vacated pegs, keeping them in the same order, and knit them. Tighten the stitches to prevent elongated stitches.

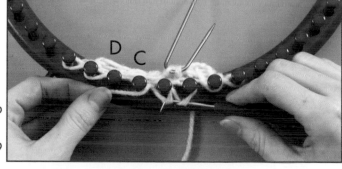

Fig. 11g

I-CORD ·················

I-cord is a narrow tube of knitting. It is used as a handle on the Felted Basketweave Tote on page 42. It is also attached as an edging to the Sampler Afghan on page 37 as it is being formed.

You can work circular on a 6 peg spool loom or on the end of a straight loom using a loom clip to form a small circle. A circular loom is used for attaching the cord to the afghan. You can also use the end of a straight loom without a clip as follows:

Using the pegs at the end of a straight loom, chain cast on 6 pegs **clockwise** (*Fig. 5e, page 11*).

★ Do **not** work back in the other direction. Instead, bring the working yarn across the inside of the loom, then to the outside between the first and second pegs cast on (*Fig. 12a*). Working a right to left row, e-wrap knit all of the pegs counter-clockwise (*Fig. 12b*); repeat from ★ until length indicated in instructions is obtained, giving the cord a tug every few rows pulling the stitches until they look evenly worked (*Fig. 12c*).

Work chain one bind off (*Figs. 9a-c, page 16*).

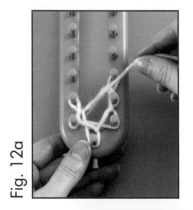
Fig. 12a

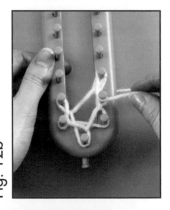
Fig. 12b

Fig. 12c

DECREASES ·················

All of the decreases are basically the same and use 2 pegs. A loop is moved to the peg next to it and then both loops are worked as one. What makes them different is which stitch is placed on top and whether the stitch is then knit or e-wrapped when worked together.

LEFT DECREASE
Use the tool to move the loop from peg A to the **left** and place it on peg B, leaving peg A empty (*Fig. 13a*). Knit peg B, lifting the bottom 2 loops over the working yarn and off the peg (*Fig. 13b*).

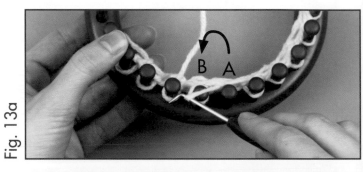
Fig. 13a

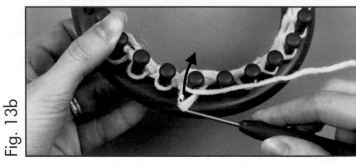
Fig. 13b

LEFT E-WRAP DECREASE
Use the tool to move the loop from peg A to the **left** and place it on peg B, leaving peg A empty *(Fig. 13a)*. E-wrap peg B *(Fig. 13c)* and lift the bottom 2 loops over the top loop and off the peg *(Fig. 13b)*.

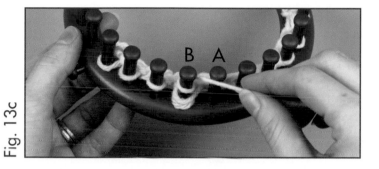

Fig. 13c

RIGHT E-WRAP DECREASE
Use the tool to move the loop from peg B to the **right** and place it on peg A, leaving peg B empty *(Fig. 13d)*. E-wrap peg A *(Fig. 13f)* and lift the bottom 2 loops over the top loop and off the peg *(Fig. 13e)*.

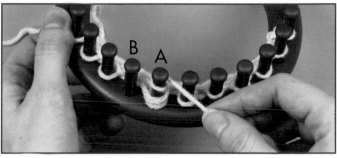

Fig. 13f

RIGHT DECREASE
Use the tool to move the loop from peg B to the **right** and place it on peg A, leaving peg B empty *(Fig. 13d)*. Knit peg A, lifting the bottom 2 loops over the working yarn and off the peg *(Fig. 13e)*.

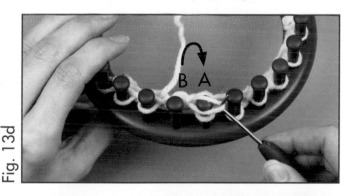

Fig. 13d

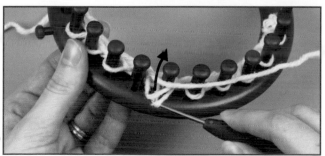

Fig. 13e

TIP
When decreasing the first or last stitch of a row for shaping, work the specified decrease. If it leaves an empty peg between the decrease and the work, move the new loop over to the empty peg.

LACE KNITTING ·······························

Lace knitting is made up of a combination of a decrease and placing the yarn around the newly empty peg *(abbreviated YRP)*, forming a lace pattern or buttonhole. The YRP is the same as an e-wrap. The new loop is not worked until the next row or round.

How the combination is worked depends on the direction you are working and which decrease is required.

To learn how to make the different decrease YRP combinations, chain cast on *(page 10)* 12 pegs onto any loom and knit one row *(page 6)*.

ON A LEFT TO RIGHT ROW
One easy combination is the "left decrease, YRP".

LEFT DECREASE, YRP
Work left decrease in the normal way *(Figs. 13a & b, page 20)*. E-wrap the empty peg (peg A) clockwise to create the YRP *(Fig. 14a)*.

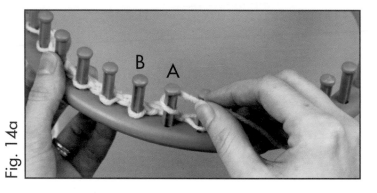

Fig. 14a

Sometimes it is necessary to change the position of the stitches to create an empty peg before or after the decrease in order to be able to work the needed combination. Work as indicated in the individual instructions.

YRP, LEFT DECREASE
Skip the next peg (peg B) and remove the loop from the next peg (peg A) using your fingers. Using the tool, move the loop from the skipped peg to the empty peg *(Fig. 14b)*, then place the loop you are holding on top of the loop you just moved. E-wrap the empty peg clockwise to create the YRP, and bring the yarn to the outside *(Fig. 14c)*. Knit the next peg (peg A) lifting the bottom 2 loops over the working yarn and off the peg to create the decrease.

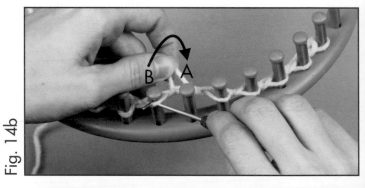

Fig. 14b

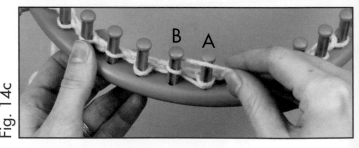

Fig. 14c

Note: The "YRP, left e-wrap decrease" is worked the same as above, only e-wrapping the peg in place of knitting the peg *(Fig. 13c, page 21)*.

YRP, RIGHT DECREASE

Use the tool to move the loop from the next peg (peg B) to the peg on the right (peg A) *(Fig. 13d, page 21)*. E-wrap the empty peg clockwise to create the YRP, and bring the yarn to the outside *(Fig. 14d)*. Knit the next peg (peg A) lifting the bottom 2 loops over the working yarn and off the peg to create the decrease *(Fig. 13e, page 21)*.

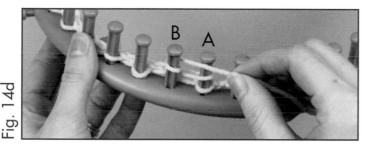

Fig. 14d

ON A RIGHT TO LEFT ROW
YRP, LEFT DECREASE

Use the tool to move the loop from the next peg (peg A) to the peg on the left (peg B). E-wrap the empty peg counter-clockwise to create the YRP, and bring the yarn to the outside. Knit the next peg lifting the bottom 2 loops over the working yarn and off the peg to create the decrease *(Fig. 14e)*.

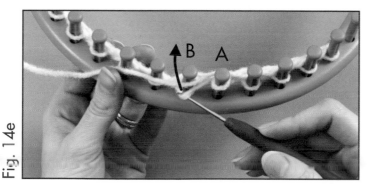

Fig. 14e

LEFT DECREASE, YRP

Remove the loop from the next peg (peg A) using your fingers. Using the tool, move the loop from the next peg (peg B) to the empty peg *(Fig. 14f)*, then place the loop you are holding on top of the loop you just moved. Knit the peg lifting the bottom 2 loops over the working yarn and off the peg to create the decrease *(Fig. 14g)*. E-wrap the empty peg counter-clockwise to create the YRP.

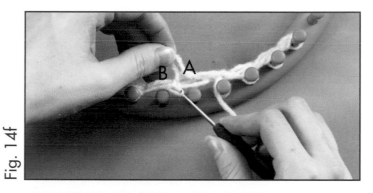

Fig. 14f

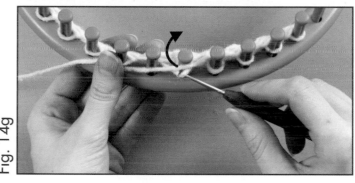

Fig. 14g

Note: The "left e-wrap decrease, YRP" is worked the same as above, only e-wrapping the peg in place of knitting the peg *(Fig. 13c, page 21)*.

SHORT ROWS & WRAPPING PEGS ....

Short rows are formed by only working across some of the pegs that have stitches on them before stopping and working back. This method adds extra length to some of the stitches for shaping that is needed for the Panda Hat, Gloves, Stocking, and Baby Blanket.

In order to prevent holes when working short rows, it is sometimes necessary to wrap the yarn around an unworked peg before changing directions. Work as instructed in the individual instructions.

To practice, either e-wrap cast on **(page 4)** or chain cast on **(page 10)** 8 pegs on any loom and knit one row.

Next Row: Knit across to last peg or across the pegs indicated in the pattern. Wrap the next peg as follows (Figs. below show working a row from left to right):

Step 1: Move the working yarn to the side and out of the way. Using the tool, lift the loop from the peg to be wrapped and hold it on the tool.

Step 2: Bring the working yarn behind the empty peg, then to the outside of the loom and across the front of the empty peg *(Fig. 15a)*.

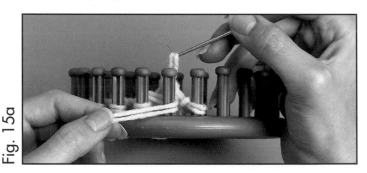

Fig. 15a

Step 3: Put the loop back onto the peg. The wrap will be under the loop *(Fig. 15b)*. Leave the remaining peg(s) unworked.

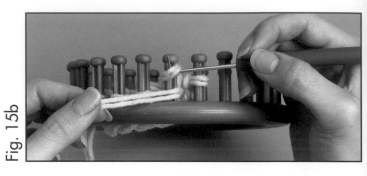

Fig. 15b

If you are using the e-wrap knit stitch method, bring the working yarn back to the inside of the loom so that it is in position to work back in the other direction.

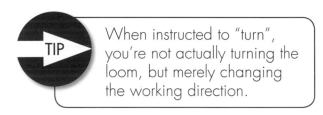

TIP — When instructed to "turn", you're not actually turning the loom, but merely changing the working direction.

You will be instructed in the pattern when to work the wrapped peg. To do so, knit or e-wrap knit the wrapped peg as specified, lifting both of the loops over the top strand or loop and off the peg.

general INSTRUCTIONS

Many terms used in loom knitting are abbreviated. This method of writing saves time and space and is actually easy to read once you understand the knitting shorthand.

ABBREVIATIONS

cm	centimeters
EWK	e-wrap knit
K	knit
mm	millimeters
P	purl
Rnd(s)	round(s)
WYIF	with yarn in front
YRP	yarn around peg

SYMBOLS AND TERMS

★ — work instructions following ★ as many **more** times as indicated in addition to the first time.

( ) or [ ] — work enclosed instructions **as many** times as specified by the number immediately following **or** contains explanatory remarks.

colon (:) — the number(s) given after a colon at the end of a row or round denote(s) the number of pegs you should have remaining on that row.

working yarn — the strand coming from the skein.

SKILL LEVELS

■□□□ BEGINNER

Beginner: Projects for first-time loom knitters using basic knit and purl stitches, and simple color changes.

■■□□ EASY

Easy: Projects using basic stitches, repetitive stitch patterns, simple color changes, and simple finishing.

■■□□ EASY +

Easy +: Projects using basic stitches, repetitive stitch patterns, simple color changes, simple short rows, and simple shaping and finishing.

■■■□ INTERMEDIATE

Intermediate: Projects with a variety of stitches such as cables and lace, also short rows, and mid-level shaping and finishing.

YARN

Yarn is divided into six basic categories. Corresponding icons are found on most yarn labels. Other names that the yarn weight may also be called are listed below.

Yarn Weight Symbol & Names	SUPER FINE 1	FINE 2	LIGHT 3	MEDIUM 4	BULKY 5	SUPER BULKY 6
Type of Yarns in Category	Sock, Fingering, Buby	Sport, Baby	DK, Light Worsted	Worsted, Afghan, Aran	Chunky, Craft, Rug	Bulky, Roving

Some projects included are made with a single strand of yarn while others are worked holding two strands of yarn together as a single strand. This is a great way to achieve wonderful results combining some of the specialty yarns available.

WINDING YARN INTO A BALL

Many yarns come in "pull-skeins," where the yarn is pulled from the center of the skein. In this form, it is easy to keep clean and less likely to tangle or unwind too quickly. Other yarns are sold in hanks that must be wound into balls before they are ready for use. Remove the label and unfold the hank to form a circle. Slip the yarn over the back of a chair and cut the knot that holds the strands together. Gently wrap the yarn around two fingers and continue to wind the yarn very loosely, rotating to keep the ball uniform. Be careful to wind the ball loosely. If the yarn is pulled too tightly or stretched while being wound, it will lose some of its elasticity.

GAUGE

Gauge is the number of stitches and rows in every inch of your knitting and is used to control the finished size. Exact gauge is essential for proper size. Before beginning your project, make a sample swatch approximately 4" (10 cm) wide with the yarn and loom specified in the individual instructions. After completing the swatch, give it a tug, holding the cast on and bound off edges, then let it "rest."
Measure it, counting your stitches and rows carefully. If your swatch is larger or smaller than specified, make another, changing your tension of the working yarn as you form the stitches. Keep trying until you find the tension you need to achieve gauge. Maintain established gauge throughout project.

WEAVING SEAMS

With the **right** side of both pieces facing you and edges even, sew through both sides once to secure the seam. Insert the needle under the bar between the first and second stitches on the row and pull the yarn through (*Fig. 16*). Insert the needle under the next bar on the second side. Repeat from side to side, being careful to match rows. If the edges are different lengths, it may be necessary to insert the needle under two bars at one edge.

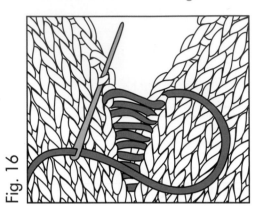

Fig. 16

BLOCKING

All pieces that are to be sewn together should be blocked beforehand to acheive the best results. Also block lace and cable patterns. Acrylics can be blocked by wetting and pinning the piece with rust-proof pins to the correct measurement. Cover it with a damp cotton cloth (kitchen towel) and hold a steam iron over the top (without touching) to heat the knitted fabric. Remember not to touch the iron to the piece as acrylic will melt.

FELTING

Felting happens when you do what Mother told you not to do to your wool sweaters—wash them in hot water! Wool will shrink and the stitches melt together to become a solid piece of felted cloth when agitated in hot water.

The felting projects in this leaflet use yarns with 100% wool content. Use a yarn with at least 80% wool content. Using a yarn with a higher wool content will make the felting process more successful. If a wool yarn is titled as super washed, it will **not** felt.

To felt your knitted project, place it in a zippered pillowcase or lingerie bag. Toss it into your washer with a pair of jeans and a small amount of detergent. Wash project in hot water on the regular cycle to agitate. Set a timer for 3 to 5 minutes so that you can check the felting progress. Please remember this is hot water! Use caution when checking the project so that you do not scald your hands. When you stretch the knitting and are unable to see the defined stitches, the project is felted. Continue setting timer for 3 minute intervals and checking the felting progress until it is completed. **Watch it carefully! The longer the project is in the washer, the more it shrinks!**

Once the project is felted, remove it from the washer, hand rinse in warm water, and pat dry with a towel. Do **not** put your project in the dryer, as it will continue to shrink and change its shape. Shape the project over an item the same shape and size of your piece and allow to air dry. This may take several days.

BASIC CROCHET STITCHES

SLIP KNOT

Make a circle and place the working yarn under the circle *(Fig. 17a)*. Insert a crochet hook under the bar just made *(Fig. 17b)* or pick up the bar with your fingers and pull on both ends of the yarn to complete the slip knot forming a loop *(Fig. 17c)*.

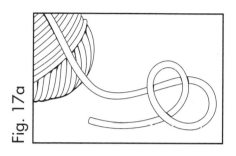

Fig. 17a

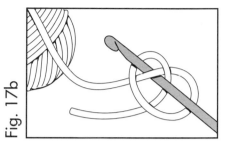

Fig. 17b

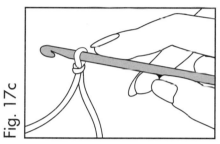

Fig. 17c

YARN OVER

Bring the yarn over the top of the hook from back to front, catching the yarn with the hook and turning the hook slightly toward you to keep the yarn from slipping off *(Fig. 18)*.

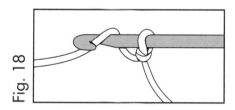

Fig. 18

CHAIN

Yarn over *(Fig. 18)*, draw the yarn through the loop on the hook *(Fig. 19)*.

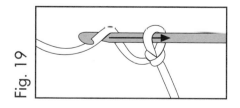

Fig. 19

SAMPLER AFGHAN ....

This is a learn-as-you-go afghan. The Squares are presented in order of difficulty with skills ranging from beginner to intermediate. You will quickly develop new skills with each Square you make.

Finished Size: 36¹/₂" x 48¹/₂" (92.5 cm x 123 cm)

MATERIALS

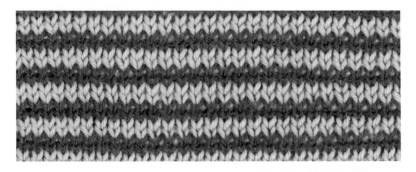

Medium Weight Yarn

[4 ounces, 186 yards
(113 grams, 170 meters) per skein]:
  Color A (Brown) - 3 skeins
  Color B (Teal) - 2 skeins
  Color C (Lt Teal) - 1 skein
48 Peg round loom
Knitting loom tool
Crochet hook, size K (6.5 mm)
Cable needle
Yarn needle

This afghan is made up of 12 Squares, each worked in a different pattern stitch, perfect for learning new stitches. Each Square is worked as flat knitting and should measure approximately 12" (30.5 cm) once blocked.

GAUGE: 11 Knit stitches = 3½" (9 cm);
        21 rows = 4" (10 cm)

When changing colors, do **not** cut the yarn; drop the color that you are working with to the inside of the loom. Then pick up the next color from underneath the strand **(Fig. 7d, page 13)**.

A. STOCKINETTE STITCH

This is the easiest of the pattern stitches because it only uses the knit stitch. It is the most basic fabric in knitting.

With Color B, chain cast on 38 pegs **(Figs. 5a-d, pages 10 & 11)**, placing the loop from the hook onto the last peg needed.

Row 1: Knit across **(Figs. 2a-c, page 6)**.

Rows 2 and 3: With Color C, knit across.

Rows 4 and 5: With Color B, knit across.

Rows 6-64: Repeat Rows 2-5, 14 times; then repeat Rows 2-4 once **more**.

Cut Color C.

With Color B, work chain one bind off across **(Figs. 9a-c, page 16)**.

Instructions continued on page 30.

B. TWISTED STOCKINETTE STITCH

The Twisted Stockinette Stitch is made of e-wrap knit stitches, which produces a loose weave full of texture.

With Color B, chain cast on 30 pegs.

Rows 1-4: E-wrap knit across *(Figs. 8a-f, pages 14 & 15)*.

Twist the yarn being used with the dropped yarn at the beginning of Rows 7 and 11 to prevent long strands along the edge *(Fig. 7e, page 13)*.

Rows 5-8: With Color C, e-wrap knit across.

Rows 9-12: With Color B, e-wrap knit across.

Rows 13-44: Repeat Rows 5-12, 4 times.

Cut Color C.

With Color B, work chain one bind off across.

C. CROSSED STOCKINETTE STITCH

Alternating a row of e-wrap knit stitches with a row of knit stitches results in a medium weave textured fabric.

With Color A, chain cast on 31 pegs.

Row 1: E-wrap knit across.

Row 2: Knit across.

Rows 3-53: Repeat Rows 1 and 2, 25 times; then repeat Row 1 once **more**.

Work chain one bind off across.

D. GARTER STITCH

Alternating a row of knit stitches with a row of purl stitches results in a reversible fabric that doesn't curl. It is a good choice for borders.

With Color A, chain cast on 35 pegs.

Row 1: Knit across.

Row 2: Purl across *(Figs. 6a-d, page 12)*.

Rows 3-69: Repeat Rows 1 and 2, 33 times; then repeat Row 1 once **more**.

Work chain one bind off across.

E. CORN ON THE COB

Skipping a peg with the yarn placed in **back** of the skipped peg combines two colors to form a pattern that looks like you changed colors every other stitch. Only one color is used on each row, alternating the colors every two rows. The texture is made up of knit stitches, e-wrap knit stitches, and purl stitches.

With Color B, chain cast on 36 pegs.

Row 1: Purl across.

When instructed to **skip a peg**, bring the yarn to the inside of the loom across the peg to be skipped and ready to e-wrap knit the next peg **or** back to the outside, ready to knit or purl the next peg *(Fig. 10a, page 17)*.

Row 2: With Color C, K2, (skip 1, K1) across.

Row 3: P1, (skip 1, P1) across to last 3 pegs, skip 1, P2.

Row 4: With Color B, K1, (skip 1, e-wrap K1) across to last peg, K1.

Row 5: P2, (skip 1, P1) across.

Rows 6-97: Repeat Rows 2-5, 23 times.

Cut Color C.

Row 98: With Color B, purl across.

Work chain one bind off across.

F. HONEYCOMB

When a peg is skipped and the yarn is placed in **front** of the work, the horizontal strand forms an interesting pattern.

With Color A, chain cast on 37 pegs.

Row 1: Knit across.

When instructed to **skip a peg with yarn in front (abbreviated skip 1 WYIF)**, use the tool to lift the loop from the peg to be skipped and hold it on the tool. Bring the yarn in front of the loop on the tool and behind the empty peg to the outside of the loom *(Fig. 10b, page 17)*. Put the loop on the tool back onto the peg.

Row 2: P1, (skip 1 WYIF, P1) across.

Row 3: Knit across.

Row 4: P2, (skip 1 WYIF, P1) across to last 3 pegs, skip 1 WYIF, P2.

Row 5: Knit across.

Rows 6-101: Repeat Rows 2-5, 24 times.

Work chain one bind off across.

Instructions continued on page 32.

G. DIAGONAL STOCKINETTE STITCH STRIPE

Working in Stockinette Stitch (all knit stitches), the diagonal stripe is formed by changing the sequence of the skipped pegs. One stitch at each edge is worked in Garter Stitch (alternating a knit stitch with a purl stitch on every other row).

With Color B, chain cast on 36 pegs **clockwise** *(Fig. 5e, page 11)*.

Row 1: Knit across.

When instructed to **skip peg(s)**, bring the yarn to the inside of the loom across the peg(s) to be skipped, then back to the outside, ready to knit the next stitch.

Row 2: With Color C, K1, (skip 2, K2) across to last 3 pegs, skip 2, K1.

Row 3: P1, (skip 1, K3) across to last 3 pegs, skip 1, K1, P1.

Row 4: With Color B, K1, skip 1, K2, (skip 2, K2) across.

Row 5: P1, K1, (skip 1, K3) across to last 2 pegs, skip 1, P1.

Row 6: With Color C, K3, (skip 2, K2) across to last 5 pegs, skip 2, K3.

Row 7: P1, K2, (skip 1, K3) across to last peg, P1.

Row 8: With Color B, K2, (skip 2, K2) across to last 2 pegs, skip 1, K1.

Row 9: P1, K3, (skip 1, K3) across to last 4 pegs, skip 1, K2, P1.

Rows 10-97: Repeat Rows 2-9, 11 times.

Cut Color C.

Row 98: With Color B, knit across.

Work chain one bind off across.

H. TWO-TONED LATTICE

Color B is worked in Garter Stitch and Color C is worked in Stockinette Stitch. The way that the pegs are skipped is what makes the Garter Stitches to appear to be sitting on top.

With Color B, chain cast on 32 pegs.

Row 1: Knit across.

When instructed to **skip peg(s)**, bring the yarn to the inside of the loom across the peg(s) to be skipped, then back to the outside, ready to knit or purl the next stitch.

Rows 2 and 3: With Color C, K1, skip 1, K4, (skip 2, K4) across to last 2 pegs, skip 1, K1.

Row 4: With Color B, K1, skip 1, K4, (skip 2, K4) across to last 2 pegs, skip 1, K1.

Row 5: P1, skip 1, P4, (skip 2, P4) across to last 2 pegs, skip 1, P1.

Rows 6 and 7: With Color C, K3, (skip 2, K4) across to last 5 pegs, skip 2, K3.

Row 8: With Color B, K3, (skip 2, K4) across to last 5 pegs, skip 2, K3.

Row 9: P3, (skip 2, P4) across to last 5 pegs, skip 2, P3.

Rows 10-121: Repeat Rows 2-9, 14 times.

Cut Color C.

Row 122: With Color B, knit across.

Work chain one bind off across.

I. SIMULATED BASKETWEAVE

It's possible to make color patterns simply by skipping pegs, allowing you to use one color for every two rows.

With Color B, chain cast on 35 pegs.

Row 1: Knit across.

When instructed to **skip peg(s)**, bring the yarn to the inside of the loom across the peg(s) to be skipped, then back to the outside, ready to knit the next stitch.

Row 2: With Color C, K4, (skip 2, K8) twice, skip 2, K9.

Row 3: K9, (skip 2, K8) twice, skip 2, K4.

Rows 4 and 5: With Color B, (K1, skip 1) twice, (K2, skip 1, K1, skip 1) across to last peg, K1.

Row 6: With Color C, K9, (skip 2, K8) twice, skip 2, K4.

Row 7: K4, (skip 2, K8) twice, skip 2, K9.

Row 8: With Color B, K1, (skip 1, K6, skip 1, K2) across to last 4 pegs, skip 1, K3.

Row 9: K3, (skip 1, K2, skip 1, K6) across to last 2 pegs, skip 1, K1.

Row 10: With Color C, K9, (skip 2, K8) twice, skip 2, K4.

Row 11: K4, (skip 2, K8) twice, skip 2, K9.

Rows 12 and 13: With Color B, (K1, skip 1) twice, (K2, skip 1, K1, skip 1) across to last peg, K1.

Row 14: With Color C, K4, (skip 2, K8) twice, skip 2, K9.

Row 15: K9, (skip 2, K8) twice, skip 2, K4.

Row 16: With Color B, K3, (skip 1, K2, skip 1, K6) across to last 2 pegs, skip 1, K1.

Row 17: K1, (skip 1, K6, skip 1, K2) across to last 4 pegs, skip 1, K3.

Rows 18-81: Repeat Rows 2-17, 4 times.

Cut Color C.

Row 82: With Color B, knit across.

Work chain one bind off across.

Instructions continued on page 34.

J. SEED STITCH & CABLES

Seed Stitch is a reversible knit and purl combination that works well as a border because it will lay flat. Here it surrounds two groups of eight stitches with the center four stitches of each changing places every four rows to form the cables.

Right   Left

TIP After working the first row, a good trick to remember the Seed Stitch pattern is to knit the purl stitches and purl the knit stitches.

STITCH GUIDE ....

LEFT CROSS CABLE (uses next 4 pegs)
Bring the working yarn to the inside of the loom, across the next 2 pegs, then back to the outside and **loosely** knit the next 2 pegs, then place them onto a cable needle, and let it hang at the inside of the loom. Bring the working yarn to the inside of the loom, and across all 4 pegs, then to the outside before the first skipped peg. Knit the 2 skipped pegs, then move them to the empty pegs, keeping them in the same order. Place the stitches from the cable needle onto the newly vacated pegs, keeping them in the same order **(Figs. 11a-e, pages 18 & 19)**. Tighten the stitches to prevent elongated stitches.

RIGHT CROSS CABLE (uses next 4 pegs)
Place the stitches from the next 2 pegs onto a cable needle and let it hang at the inside of the loom. Bring the working yarn behind the 2 empty pegs and to the outside of the loom. Knit the next 2 pegs, then use the tool to move them to the empty pegs, keeping them in the same order. With the working yarn outside the loom, place the stitches from the cable needle onto the newly vacated pegs, keeping them in the same order, and knit them **(Figs. 11f & g, page 19)**. Tighten the stitches to prevent elongated stitches.

With Color A, chain cast on 40 pegs **clockwise**.

Rows 1-3: ★ K1, (P1, K1) 3 times, P3, K4, P2; repeat from ★ once **more**, (K1, P1) 4 times.

Row 4: K1, (P1, K1) 3 times, P3, work Left Cross Cable, P2, K1, (P1, K1) 3 times, P3, work Right Cross Cable, P2, (K1, P1) 4 times.

Rows 5-59: Repeat Rows 1-4, 13 times; then repeat Rows 1-3 once **more**.

Work chain one bind off across.

K. RIDGED LACE

Using a combination of Garter Stitch and lace makes a light and airy texture.

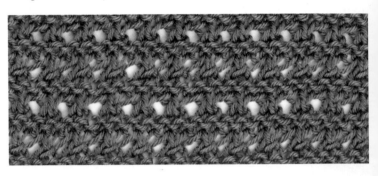

STITCH GUIDE ....

YRP, RIGHT DECREASE

Move the loop from the next peg to the peg on the right **(Fig. 13d, page 21)**. E-wrap the empty peg clockwise to create the YRP, and bring the yarn to the outside **(Fig. 14d, page 23)**. Knit the next peg lifting the bottom 2 loops over the working yarn and off the peg to create the decrease **(Fig. 13e page 21)**.

YRP, LEFT DECREASE

Skip the next peg and remove the loop from the next peg using your fingers. Move the loop from the skipped peg to the empty peg **(Fig. 14b, page 22)**, then place the loop you are holding on top of the loop you just moved. E-wrap the empty peg clockwise to create the YRP, and bring the yarn to the outside **(Fig. 14c, page 22)**. Knit the next peg lifting the bottom 2 loops over the working yarn and off the peg to create the decrease.

With Color A, chain cast on 31 pegs.

Row 1: Knit across.

Row 2: Purl across.

Row 3: Knit across.

Row 4: K1, (YRP, right decrease) across.

Row 5: Knit across.

Row 6: Purl across.

Row 7: Knit across.

Row 8: K1, (YRP, left decrease) across.

Rows 9-59: Repeat Rows 1-8, 6 times; then repeat Rows 1-3 once **more**.

Work chain one bind off across.

L. SNAKES & LADDERS LACE

This lace pattern is formed by moving the placement of the decrease and the yarn around peg combination every row.

STITCH GUIDE ....
LEFT DECREASE, YRP
Skip the next peg and move the loop from the next peg to the skipped peg. Knit the peg lifting the bottom 2 loops over the working yarn and off the peg to create the decrease *(Figs. 13a & b, page 20)*. E-wrap the empty peg clockwise to create the YRP *(Fig. 14a, page 22)*, and bring the yarn to the outside.

YRP, LEFT DECREASE
Move the loop from the next peg to the peg on the left. E-wrap the empty peg counter-clockwise to create the YRP, and bring the yarn to the outside. Knit the next peg lifting the bottom 2 loops over the working yarn and off the peg to create the decrease *(Fig. 14e, page 23)*.

LEFT E-WRAP DECREASE, YRP
Remove the loop from the next peg using your fingers. Move the loop from the next peg to the empty peg, then place the loop you are holding on top of the loop you just moved *(Fig. 14f, page 23)*. E-wrap knit the peg lifting the bottom 2 loops over the top loop and off the peg to create the decrease. E-wrap the empty peg counter-clockwise to create the YRP, and bring the yarn to the outside.

YRP, LEFT E-WRAP DECREASE
Skip the next peg and remove the loop from the next peg using your fingers. Move the loop from the skipped peg to the empty peg *(Fig. 14b, page 22)*, then place the loop you are holding on top of the loop you just moved. E-wrap the empty peg clockwise to create the YRP, and bring the yarn to the outside *(Fig. 14c, page 22)*. E-wrap knit the next peg lifting the bottom 2 loops over the top loop and off the peg to create the decrease.

With Color A, chain cast on 34 pegs.

Row 1: Knit across.

Row 2: K7, left decrease, YRP, (K6, left decrease, YRP) across to last peg, K1.

Instructions continued on page 36.

Row 3: P2, (YRP, left decrease, P6) across.

Row 4: K5, left decrease, YRP, (K6, left decrease, YRP) across to last 3 pegs, K3.

Row 5: P4, YRP, left decrease, (P6, YRP, left decrease) across to last 4 pegs, P4.

Row 6: K3, left decrease, YRP, (K6, left decrease, YRP) across to last 5 pegs, K5.

Row 7: (P6, YRP, left decrease) across to last 2 pegs, P2.

Row 8: K1, left decrease, YRP, (K6, left decrease, YRP) across to last 7 pegs, K7.

Row 9: P7, left e-wrap decrease, YRP, (P6, left e-wrap decrease, YRP) across to last peg, P1.

Row 10: K2, (YRP, left e-wrap decrease, K6) across.

Row 11: P5, left e-wrap decrease, YRP, (P6, left e-wrap decrease, YRP) across to last 3 pegs, P3.

Row 12: K4, YRP, left e-wrap decrease, (K6, YRP, left e-wrap decrease) across to last 4 pegs, K4.

Row 13: P3, left e-wrap decrease, YRP, (P6, left e-wrap decrease, YRP) across to last 5 pegs, P5.

Row 14: (K6, YRP, left e-wrap decrease) across to last 2 pegs, K2.

Row 15: P1, left e-wrap decrease, YRP, (P6, left e-wrap decrease, YRP) across to last 7 pegs, P7.

Rows 16-57: Repeat Rows 2-15, 3 times.

Row 58: Knit across.

Work chain one bind off across.

FINISHING
Block each Square to 12" x 12" (30.5 cm x 30.5 cm) *(see Blocking, page 26)*.

With Color A and using Placement Diagram as a guide, sew Squares together, forming 3 vertical strips of 4 Squares each. Sew strips together in same manner.

Placement Diagram

L	A	F
I	J	H
C	B	K
G	D	E

ATTACHED I-CORD EDGING

Using Color B, moving around the loom to your left, and wrapping each peg counter-clockwise, e-wrap cast on 4 pegs.

Bring the afghan into the center of the loom with the **right** side facing the pegs. Pick up a stitch by inserting the crochet hook through any stitch from **front** to **back** *(Fig. 20a)*. Catching the working yarn with the hook, bring it back through the knitting *(Fig. 20b)*. Twist the loop and place it on the next empty peg *(Fig. 20c)*.

★ Do **not** work back in the other direction. Instead, bring the working yarn along the inside of the loom, to the first peg that was worked. E-wrap knit the pegs in the same direction as the previous row *(Fig. 20d)*.

Fig. 20d

Fig. 20a

Fig. 20b

Fig. 20c

Pick up a stitch in the next stitch of the afghan; twist the loop and place it on the last peg that has a stitch. Knit it by lifting the bottom loop over the top loop and off the peg.

Repeat from ★ around the afghan picking up a stitch in every stitch along the top and the bottom of the afghan and in every other row along the sides. When rounding the corners of the afghan, pick up an extra stitch in each of the corner stitches.

When you reach the starting point, work chain one bind off.

Sew ends of Edging together.

Weave in yarn ends.

CORN ON THE COB HAT & SCARF SET .

◀◼◻◻ **EASY**

Finished Sizes:
Hat - Fits most adults
Scarf - 4½" x 66" (11.5 cm x 167.5 cm)

MATERIALS
Medium Weight Yarn
[3.5 ounces, 170 yards
(100 grams, 156 meters) per skein]:
    Color A (Rust) - 2 skeins
    Color B (Gold) - 2 skeins
Straight looms:
    50 Peg loom for Hat
    38 Peg loom for Scarf
Knitting loom tool
Crochet hook, size K (6.5 mm)
Yarn needle

When instructed to **skip a peg**, bring the yarn to the inside of the loom across the peg to be skipped, and ready to e-wrap knit the next peg **or** back to the outside, ready to knit or purl the next peg **(Fig. 10a, page 17)**.

When changing colors, do **not** cut the yarn; drop the color that you are working with to the inside of the loom. Then pick up the next color from underneath the strand **(Figs. 7c & d, page 13)**.

HAT

GAUGE: In pattern,
        8 stitches and 28 rows = 3" (7.5 cm)

With Color A and working as circular knitting, chain cast on 50 pegs.

Rnd 1: Purl around; drop yarn to the inside of the loom.

Rnd 2: With Color B and placing the beginning yarn end at the inside of the loom, (K1, skip 1) around.

Rnd 3: (P1, skip 1) around.

Rnd 4: With Color A, (skip 1, e-wrap K1) around.

Rnd 5: (Skip 1, P1) around.

Rnds 6-73: Repeat Rows 2-5, 17 times.

Cut Color B.

Rnd 74: With Color A, knit around.

Cut Color A leaving a 18" (45.5 cm) length for sewing.

Work Gathered Removal to remove Hat from loom and to close top of Hat **(Figs. 3a & b, page 7)**.

SCARF

GAUGE: In pattern,
16 stitches and 36 rows =
4½" (11.5 cm)

With Color A and working as flat knitting, chain cast on 16 pegs.

Row 1: Purl across; drop yarn to the inside of the loom.

Row 2: With Color B and placing the beginning yarn end at the inside of the loom, K2, (skip 1, K1) across.

Row 3: P1, (skip 1, P1) across to last 3 pegs, skip 1, P2.

Row 4: With Color A, K1, (skip 1, e wrap K1) across to last peg, K1.

Row 5: P2, (skip 1, P1) across.

Repeat Rows 2-5 for pattern until Scarf measures approximately 65½" (166.5 cm) from cast on edge.

Cut Color B.

Last Row: With Color A, purl across.

Work chain one bind off across *(Figs. 9a-c, page 16)*.

Weave in yarn ends.

HONEYCOMB HAT & SCARF SET ·········

■■□□ EASY +

Finished Sizes:
Hat - Fits most adults
Scarf - 4¾" x 22½" (12 cm x 57 cm)

MATERIALS
Bulky Weight Yarn **⑤ BULKY**
[3.5 ounces, 109 yards
(100 grams, 100 meters) per skein]:
  2 skeins
48 Peg round loom
Knitting loom tool
Crochet hook, size K (6.5 mm)
Yarn needle
1⅛" (28 mm) Buttons - 2
Sewing needle and matching thread

When instructed to **skip a peg with yarn in front (abbreviated skip 1 WYIF)**, use the tool to lift the loop from the peg to be skipped and hold it on the tool. Bring the yarn behind the empty peg, then around the peg to the outside of the loom **(Fig. 10b, page 17)**. Put the loop that is on the tool back onto the peg.

HAT

GAUGE: In pattern,
        10 stitches and 28 rows = 4" (10 cm)

Working as circular knitting, chain cast on 48 pegs.

Rnd 1: Knit around.

Rnd 2: (Skip 1 WYIF, P1) around.

Rnd 3: Knit around.

Rnd 4: (P1, skip 1 WYIF) around.

Rnds 5-56: Repeat Rnds 1-4, 13 times.

Cut yarn leaving a 18" (45.5 cm) length for sewing.

Work Gathered Removal to remove Hat from loom and to close top of Hat **(Figs. 3a & b, page 7)**.

SCARF

GAUGE: In pattern,
        14 stitches and 26 rows = 4" (10 cm)

STITCH GUIDE ······································
LEFT DECREASE, YRP
Remove the loop from the next peg using your fingers. Move the loop from the next peg to the empty peg **(Fig. 14f, page 23)**, then place the loop you are holding on top of the loop you just moved. Knit the peg lifting the bottom 2 loops over the working yarn and off the peg to create the decrease **(Fig. 14g, page 23)**. E-wrap the empty peg counter-clockwise to create the YRP, and bring the yarn to the outside.

YRP, LEFT DECREASE
Move the loop from the next peg to the peg on the left. E-wrap the empty peg counter-clockwise to create the YRP, and bring the yarn to the outside. Knit the next peg lifting the bottom 2 loops over the working yarn and off the peg to create the decrease **(Fig. 14e, page 23)**.

Working as flat knitting, chain cast on 17 pegs.

Skip the first peg of every row to form a nice edge. Bring the yarn to the inside of the loom across the first peg, then back to the outside, ready to work the next stitch *(Fig. 10a, page 17)*.

Row 1: Skip 1, knit across.

Row 2: Skip 1, P1, (skip 1 WYIF, P1) across to last peg, K1.

Row 3: Skip 1, knit across.

Row 4: Skip 1, P2, (skip 1 WYIF, P1) across to last 4 pegs, skip 1 WYIF, P2, K1.

Rows 5-130: Repeat Rows 1-4, 31 times; then repeat Rows 1 and 2 once **more**.

Row 131 (Buttonhole row): Skip 1, K3, left decrease, YRP, K5, YRP, left decrease, K4.

Row 132: Skip 1, P2, (skip 1 WYIF, P1) across to last 4 pegs, skip 1 WYIF, P2, K1.

Rows 133-136: Repeat Rows 1-4.

Work chain one bind off across.

Weave in yarn ends.

Block Scarf *(see Blocking, page 26)*.

Using photo as a guide for placement, overlap the scarf and sew buttons in place to correspond with buttonholes.

FELTED BASKETWEAVE TOTE ....

⬤▬◻◻ EASY +

Finished Size: approximately 9" x 14"
(23 cm x 35.5 cm) after felting

MATERIALS
Medium Weight 100% Wool Yarn
[8 ounces, 465 yards
(227 grams, 425 meters) per skein]:
  Color A (Brown) - 1 skein
  Color B (Ecru) - 1 skein
62 Peg straight loom
Knitting loom tool
Crochet hook, size K (6.5 mm)
Yarn needle

Gauge is not important in felted items, since there are so many variables in the felting process.

Tote is worked as flat knitting holding two strands of yarn together as one throughout (pull one strand from the center and one from the outside of the skein).

BODY
With Color B, working as flat knitting and beginning with first peg on long side, chain cast on 55 pegs.

Row 1: Knit across; drop yarn to the inside of the loom.

When instructed to **skip peg(s)**, bring the yarn to the inside of the loom, across the peg(s) to be skipped, then back to the outside, ready to knit the next stitch *(Fig. 10a, page 17)*.

Row 2: With Color A and placing the beginning yarn end at the inside of the loom, K4, (skip 2, K8) 4 times, skip 2, K9.

Row 3: K9, (skip 2, K8) across to last 6 pegs, skip 2, K4.

Rows 4 and 5: With Color B *(Fig. 7d, page 13)*, (K1, skip 1) twice, (K2, skip 1, K1, skip 1) across to last peg, K1.

Row 6: With Color A, K9, (skip 2, K8) across to last 6 pegs, skip 2, K4.

Row 7: K4, (skip 2, K8) 4 times, skip 2, K9.

Row 8: With Color B, K1, (skip 1, K6, skip 1, K2) across to last 4 pegs, skip 1, K3.

Row 9: K3, (skip 1, K2, skip 1, K6) across to last 2 pegs, skip 1, K1.

Row 10: With Color A, K9, (skip 2, K8) across to last 6 pegs, skip 2, K4.

Row 11: K4, (skip 2, K8) 4 times, skip 2, K9.

Rows 12 and 13: With Color B, (K1, skip 1) twice, (K2, skip 1, K1, skip 1) across to last peg, K1.

Row 14: With Color A, K4, (skip 2, K8) 4 times, skip 2, K9.

Row 15: K9, (skip 2, K8) across to last 6 pegs, skip 2, K4.

Row 16: With Color B, K3, (skip 1, K2, skip 1, K6) across to last 2 pegs, skip 1, K1.

Row 17: K1, (skip 1, K6, skip 1, K2) across to last 4 pegs, skip 1, K3.

Rows 18-177: Repeat Rows 2-17, 10 times.

Cut Color A.

Row 178: With Color B, knit across.

Work chain one bind off across.

HANDLE (Make 2)

With Color A, chain cast on 6 pegs **clockwise** (*Fig. 5e, page 11*).

Work 20" (51 cm) of I-cord (*Figs. 12a-c, page 20*).

Work chain one bind off across.

FINISHING

Fold Body in half matching cast on and bound off edges and weave side seams (*Fig. 16, page 26*).

Using the diagram as a guide, fold up corners, forming the bottom and sew in place.

Using photo as a guide for placement, sew each end of Handles to **wrong** side of Tote.

Weave in yarn ends.

Felt and shape (*see Felting, page 27*).

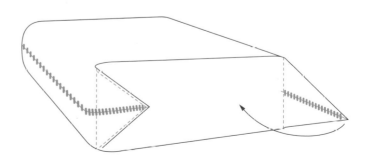

HOODED VEST ·····························

EASY +

Size	Chest	Finished Chest Measurement
Small	32/34	37" (94 cm)
Medium	36/38	40" (101.5 cm)
Large	40/42	44" (112 cm)
Extra Large	44/46	48" (122 cm)

Size Note: Instructions are written for adult size Small with sizes Medium, Large, and Extra Large in braces { }. Instructions will be easier to read if you circle all the numbers pertaining to your size. If only one number is given, it applies to all sizes.

MATERIALS

Bulky Weight Yarn **(5 BULKY)**
[3.5 ounces, 121 yards
(100 grams, 110 meters) per skein]:
  6{7-7-8} skeins
62 Peg straight loom
Knitting loom tool
Crochet hook, size K (6.5 mm)
Yarn needle
¾" (19 mm) Shank button

GAUGE: In e-wrap knit stitch,
        12 stitches and 17 rows = 4" (10 cm)

All pieces are worked as flat knitting. The Back and the Hood are worked in two separate pieces, then woven together. Always cast on counter-clockwise so that the Garter Stitch Bands and the shaping will be on the correct side.

LEFT BACK

Chain cast on 29{31-34-37} pegs.

Row 1: Purl across.

Row 2: E-wrap knit across.

Row 3: Purl across.

Repeat Row 2 until Back measures approximately 12½{13-13-13½}"/32{33-33-34.5} cm from cast on edge, ending with working yarn on the left edge of the work.

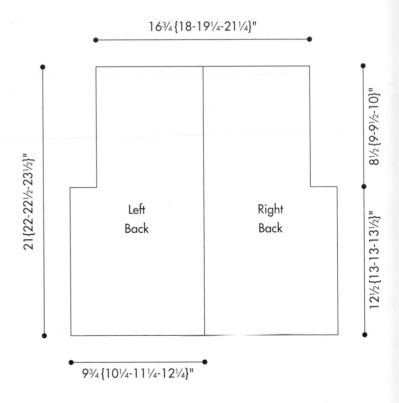

Instructions continued on page 46.

Row 4: E-wrap knit across to last 4 pegs, P3, EWK 1.

Skip the first peg of rows indicated to form a nice edge along the Armhole. Bring the yarn to the inside of the loom across the peg to be skipped *(Fig. 10a, page 17)*.

Row 5: Skip 1, e-wrap knit across.

Row 6: E-wrap knit across to last 4 pegs, P3, EWK 1.

Repeat Rows 5 and 6 until Armhole measures approximately 8½{9-9½-10}"/21.5{23-24-25.5} cm, ending by working Row 6.

SHOULDER SHAPING
Row 1: Chain one bind off 14{15-16-18} pegs, e-wrap knit across: 10{11-12-13} pegs remaining.

Row 2: E-wrap knit across.

Work chain one bind off across.

RIGHT BACK
Work same as Left Back to Armhole Shaping, ending with working yarn on the right edge of the work.

ARMHOLE SHAPING
Row 1: Chain one bind off 4{4-5-5} pegs, e-wrap knit across: 25{27-29-32} pegs remaining.

Row 2: E-wrap knit across to last 5 pegs, P3, right e-wrap decrease *(Fig. 13f, page 21)*: 24{26-28-31} pegs remaining.

Row 3: Skip 1, e-wrap knit across.

Row 4: E-wrap knit across to last 4 pegs, P3, EWK 1.

Repeat Rows 3 and 4 until Armhole measures same as Left Back to Shoulder Shaping, ending by working Row 4.

ARMHOLE SHAPING
Row 1: Chain one bind off 4{4-5-5} pegs *(Figs. 9a-c, page 16)*, e-wrap knit across: 25{27-29-32} pegs remaining.

Row 2: E-wrap knit across to last 5 pegs, P3, EWK 2.

Row 3: Left e-wrap decrease *(Fig. 13c, page 21)*, e-wrap knit across: 24{26-28-31} pegs remaining.

The decrease will leave an empty peg between it and the work. Move the new loop to the empty peg.

SHOULDER SHAPING

Row 1: Chain one bind off 14{15-16-18} pegs, e-wrap knit across: 10{11-12-13} pegs remaining.

Row 2: E-wrap knit across.

Work chain one bind off across.

RIGHT FRONT

Chain cast on 29{31-34-37} pegs.

Row 1: Purl across.

Row 2: E-wrap knit across.

Row 3: Purl across.

Row 4: E-wrap knit across.

Row 5: Skip 1, P3, e-wrap knit across.

Repeat Rows 4 and 5 until Right Front measures same as Back to Armhole Shaping, ending by working Row 5.

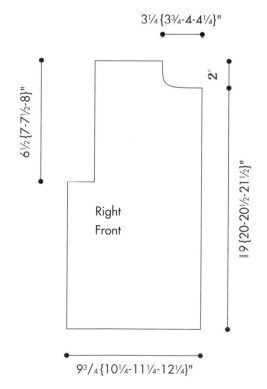

3¼ {3¾-4-4¼}"

2"

6½{7-7½-8}"

19{20-20½-21½}"

Right Front

9¾{10¼-11¼-12¼}"

ARMHOLE SHAPING

Row 1: Chain one bind off 4{4-5-5} pegs, e-wrap knit across: 25{27-29-32} pegs remaining.

Row 2: Skip 1, P3, e-wrap knit across to last 5 pegs, P3, left e-wrap decrease: 24{26-28-31} pegs remaining.

Row 3: Skip 1, e-wrap knit across.

Row 4: Skip 1, P3, e-wrap knit across to last 4 pegs, P3, EWK 1.

Repeat Rows 3 and 4 until Armhole measures approximately 6½{7-7½-8}"/16.5{18-19-20.5} cm, ending by working Row 3.

NECK SHAPING

Row 1: Chain one bind off 8{9-10-11} pegs, e-wrap knit across to last 4 pegs, P3, EWK 1: 16{17-18-20} pegs remaining.

Row 2: Skip 1, e-wrap knit across to last 2 pegs, e-wrap right decrease: 15{16-17-19} pegs remaining.

Row 3: E-wrap right decrease, e-wrap knit across to last 4 pegs, P3, EWK 1: 14{15-16-18} pegs remaining.

Row 4: Skip 1, e-wrap knit across.

Row 5: E-wrap knit across to last 4 pegs, P3, EWK 1.

Repeat Rows 4 and 5 until Armhole measures same as Back, ending by working Row 4.

Work chain one bind off across.

LEFT FRONT

Chain cast on 29{31-34-37} pegs.

Row 1: Purl across.

Row 2: E-wrap knit across.

Row 3: Purl across.

Instructions continued on page 48.

Row 4: Skip 1, e-wrap knit across.

Row 5: E-wrap knit across to last 4 pegs, P3, EWK 1.

Repeat Rows 4 and 5 until Left Front measures same as Back to Armhole Shaping, ending by working Row 4.

ARMHOLE SHAPING
Row 1: Chain one bind off 4{4-5-5} pegs, e-wrap knit across to last 4 pegs, P3, EWK 1: 25{27-29-32} pegs remaining.

Row 2: Skip 1, e-wrap knit across to last 5 pegs, P3, e-wrap right decrease: 24{26-28-31} pegs remaining.

Row 3: Skip 1, e-wrap knit across to last 4 pegs, P3, EWK 1.

Repeat Row 3 until Armhole measures same as Right Front to Neck Shaping, ending with working yarn on the left edge of the work.

NECK SHAPING
Row 1: Chain one bind off 8{9-10-11} pegs, e-wrap knit across to last 4 pegs, P3, EWK 1: 16{17-18-20} pegs remaining.

Row 2: Skip 1, e-wrap knit across to last 2 pegs, left e-wrap decrease: 15{16-17-19} pegs remaining.

Row 3: Left e-wrap decrease, e-wrap knit across to last 4 pegs, P3, EWK 1: 14{15-16-18} pegs remaining.

Row 4: Skip 1, e-wrap knit across.

Row 5: E-wrap knit across to last 4 pegs, P3, EWK 1.

Repeat Rows 4 and 5 until Armhole measures same as Back, ending by working Row 5.

Work chain one bind off across.

RIGHT HOOD
Chain cast on 35 pegs.

Row 1: E-wrap knit across.

Row 2: Purl across.

Rows 3 and 4: Repeat Rows 1 and 2.

Rows 5-10: E-wrap knit across.

Row 11: E-wrap knit across to last 2 pegs, left e-wrap decrease: 34 pegs remaining.

Rows 12-20: E-wrap knit across.

Row 21: E-wrap knit across to last 2 pegs, left e-wrap decrease: 33 pegs remaining.

Rows 22-30: E-wrap knit across.

Note: Loop a short piece of yarn around any stitch on the right edge of the work to mark top edge of Hood to be seamed.

Row 31: E-wrap knit across to last 2 pegs, left e-wrap decrease: 32 pegs remaining.

E-wrap knit every row until Right Hood measures approximately 11½" (29 cm) from cast on edge, ending with working yarn on the right edge of the work.

Work chain one bind off across.

LEFT HOOD
Chain cast on 35 pegs.

Row 1: E-wrap knit across.

Row 2: Purl across.

Rows 3 and 4: Repeat Rows 1 and 2.

Rows 5-10: E-wrap knit across

Row 11: Right e-wrap decrease, e-wrap knit across: 34 pegs remaining.

Rows 12-20: E-wrap knit across.

Row 21: Right e-wrap decrease, e-wrap knit across: 33 pegs remaining.

Rows 22-30: E-wrap knit across.

Note: Loop a short piece of yarn around any stitch on the left edge of the work to mark top edge of Hood to be seamed.

Row 31: Right e-wrap decrease, e-wrap knit across: 32 pegs remaining.

E-wrap knit every row until Left Hood measures same as Right Hood, ending with working yarn on the right edge of the work.

Work chain one bind off across.

FINISHING
Block pieces *(see Blocking, page 26)*.

Weave center Back seam *(Fig. 16, page 26)*.
Weave Fronts to Back along sides.
Sew shoulder seams.

Weave Hood pieces together along marked edges, beginning at cast on edge; fold Hood at seam and sew bound off edges together for back seam.
Sew Hood to Body, matching center seams.

Sew button to Left Front at neckline.

Button Loop: Using a crochet hook, place a slip knot on the hook, chain 7, cut yarn leaving a long end for sewing and pull end through the final loop *(see Basic Crochet Stitches, page 27)*.

Sew chain to Right Front at neck edge opposite button, forming a loop.

Weave in yarn ends.

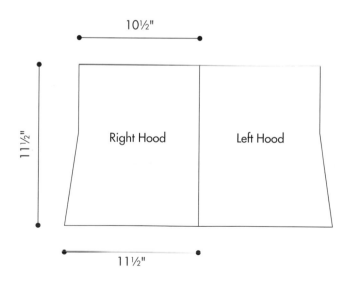

LATTICE PILLOW

■■□□ EASY +

Finished Size: 18" (45.5 cm) square

MATERIALS
Medium Weight Yarn
[4 ounces, 186 yards
(113 grams, 170 meters) per skein]:
  Color A (Brown) - 2 skeins
  Color B (Lt Teal) - 2 skeins
62 Peg straight loom
Knitting loom tool
Crochet hook, size K (6.5 mm)
Yarn needle
18" (45.5 cm) Square pillow form

GAUGE: In pattern,
       14 stitches and 32 rows = 4" (10 cm)

BODY (Make 2)
With Color A and working as flat knitting, chain cast on 62 pegs; do **not** join.

Row 1: Knit across; drop yarn to the inside of the loom.

When instructed to **skip peg(s)**, bring the yarn to the inside of the loom across the peg(s) to be skipped, then back to the outside ready to knit or purl the next stitch *(Fig. 10a, page 17)*.

Rows 2 and 3: With Color B and placing the beginning yarn end at the inside of the loom, K1, skip 1, K4, (skip 2, K4) across to last 2 pegs, skip 1, K1.

Row 4: With Color A *(Fig. 7d, page 13)*, K1, skip 1, K4, (skip 2, K4) across to last 2 pegs, skip 1, K1.

Row 5: P1, skip 1, P4, (skip 2, P4) across to last 2 pegs, skip 1, P1.

Rows 6 and 7: With Color B, K3, (skip 2, K4) across to last 5 pegs, skip 2, K3.

Row 8: With Color A, K3, (skip 2, K4) across to last 5 pegs, skip 2, K3.

Row 9: P3, (skip 2, P4) across to last 5 pegs, skip 2, P3.

Rows 10-135: Repeat Rows 2-9, 15 times; then repeat Rows 2-7 once **more**.

Cut Color B.

Row 136: With Color A, knit across.

Work chain one bind off across.

Weave in yarn ends.

Block Body *(see Blocking, page 26)*.

With **wrong** sides together, sew pieces together, inserting pillow form before closing.

BEJEWELED FINGERLESS GLOVES ....

Finished Size: fits child large to adult small

Sizing Note: The type of yarn that you use (whether it's soft or has more body) and the tension you have when you wrap the yarn, greatly effects your gauge and thus the finished size. Therefore, you can easily adjust the size of your gloves by the yarn you choose and your tension.

MATERIALS
Medium Weight Yarn
[3.5 ounces, 170 yards
(100 grams, 156 meters) per skein]:
   1 skein
38 Peg straight loom
Knitting loom tool
Loom clips - 3
6/0 Seed beads - 200 (approximately 39 grams)
Needle or floss threader
Crochet hook, size K (6.5 mm)
Yarn needle

GAUGE: In knit stitch,
          15 stitches and 24 rows = 4" (10 cm)

The fingers are knit first as circular knitting and left on the loom to be joined together when beginning the Hand.

Instructions continued on page 52.

Use the diagram for the numbering system used for this pattern.

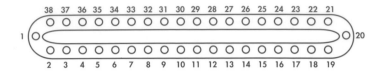

LITTLE FINGER

Place a loom clip to create a middle peg between pegs 4 and 36, with the inside curve of the clip facing the inside curve at end of loom.

Beginning with clip peg, chain cast on 6 pegs counter-clockwise, ending on peg 3.

Knit 3 rounds; cut yarn leaving a 5" (12.5 cm) length for sewing.

Transfer stitch from clip to peg 3.

RING FINGER

When using 2 clips, place them with the inside curve of the clips facing each other.

Remove clip and place it between pegs 3 and 37 and place a second clip between pegs 7 and 33.

Beginning with clip across pegs 7 and 33, chain cast on 8 pegs counter-clockwise, ending on peg 6.

Knit 3 rounds; cut yarn leaving a 5" (12.5 cm) length for sewing.

Transfer stitch from clip between pegs 7 and 33 to peg 6. Transfer stitch from clip between pegs 3 and 37 to peg 36.

MIDDLE FINGER

Remove both clips and place one between pegs 6 and 34 and a second clip between pegs 10 and 30.

Beginning with clip between pegs 6 and 34, chain cast on 8 pegs **clockwise (Fig. 5e, page 11)**, ending on peg 7.

Knit 4 rounds; cut yarn leaving a 5" (12.5 cm) length for sewing.

Transfer stitch from clip between pegs 6 and 34 to peg 33. Transfer stitch from clip between pegs 10 and 30 to peg 9.

THUMB

Remove both clips and place one between pegs 12 and 28 and a second clip between pegs 16 and 24.

Beginning with peg 13, chain cast on 8 pegs counter-clockwise, ending on clip peg.

The 3 empty pegs on each side will be left unworked for Index finger to be worked later.

Knit 3 rounds; do **not** cut yarn.

THUMB GUSSET

Begin working flat in short rows, only working across the pegs indicated. Reverse directions at the end of the written instructions for each row.

Row 1: Beginning with peg 13 and working counter-clockwise, knit across Thumb to last peg, leave last peg unworked.

Row 2: K6.

Row 3: K5.

Row 4: K4.

Row 5: K6; cut yarn leaving a 5" (12.5 cm) length for sewing.

Transfer stitch from clip between pegs 12 and 28 to peg 27.

String 200 beads onto the yarn, using the needle or floss threader. Slide the beads back on the yarn as you work until they are needed.

INDEX FINGER

Remove empty clip and place it between pegs 9 and 31. Place a third clip between pegs 13 and 27.

Beginning with peg 11, chain cast on 8 pegs counter-clockwise, ending on peg 10.

Knit 3 rounds; do **not** cut yarn.

Transfer stitch from clip between pegs 9 and 31 to peg 30; remove empty clip. Leave remaining 2 clips in place.

HAND

Mark peg 11 as first peg of each round.

Transfer top loop (leaving bottom loop in place) as follows: from peg 3 to peg 4, peg 6 to peg 7, peg 9 to peg 10, peg 30 to peg 31, peg 33 to peg 34, and peg 36 to peg 37.

When knitting a peg with 2 loops, lift the bottom 2 loops over the top loop.

Working counter-clockwise and skipping thumb pegs, knit pegs 11 and 12, knit next clip peg and each peg around: 24 pegs used.

Knit 16 rounds.

The Hand is now ready to be joined to the Thumb. Transfer stitch from clip between pegs 13 and 27 to peg 13; remove empty clip.

Transfer top loop (leaving bottom loop in place) from peg 27 to peg 28.

Two pegs will be decreased on every other round at the base of the Thumb. Move the Thumb stitches and the clip after each decrease round to avoid having empty pegs between stitches.

Rnd 1: Beginning with peg 11, knit all pegs: 30 pegs used.

Rnd 2: K1, left decrease *(Figs. 13a & b, page 20)*, K5, right decrease *(Figs. 13d & e, page 21)*, K 20: 28 pegs remaining.

Rnd 3: Knit around.

Rnd 4: K1, left decrease, K3, right decrease, K 20: 26 pegs remaining.

Rnd 5: Knit around.

Rnd 6: K1, left decrease, K1, right decrease, K 20: 24 pegs remaining.

Rnds 7 and 8: Knit around.

Add a second clip when decreasing stitches along the Little Finger side of the Glove to avoid having empty pegs between stitches.

Rnd 9: Left decrease, K1, right decrease, K7, left decrease, K1, right decrease, K7: 20 pegs remaining.

Rnds 10 and 11: Knit around.

CUFF

Rnd 1: (P1, slide 2 beads between pegs) around.

Rnd 2: P1, knit around.

Rnds 3-10: Repeat Rnds 1 and 2, 4 times.

Work chain one bind off around.

Use the yarn ends to close up holes between each finger.

Weave in yarn ends.

ROBIN'S HOOD ....

Finished Size: 10" wide x 60" long
(25.5 cm x 152.5 cm)

MATERIALS
Super Bulky Weight Yarn
[6 ounces, 106 yards
(170 grams, 97 meters) per skein]:
3 skeins
36 Peg round loom
Knitting loom tool
Crochet hook, size K (6.5 mm)
Cable needle
Yarn needle

GAUGE: In seed stitch,
10 stitches and 18 rows = 4" (10 cm)

STITCH GUIDE ....
RIGHT CROSS CABLE (uses next 4 pegs)
Place the stitches from the next 2 pegs onto a cable needle and let it hang at the inside of the loom. Bring the working yarn behind the 2 empty pegs and to the outside of the loom. Knit the next 2 pegs, then use the tool to move them to the empty pegs, keeping them in the same order. With the working yarn outside the loom, place the stitches from the cable needle onto the newly vacated pegs, keeping them in the same order, and knit them *(Figs. 11f & g, page 19)*. Tighten the stitches to prevent elongated stitches.

BODY
Working as flat knitting, chain cast on 29 pegs clockwise *(Fig. 5e, page 11)*.

Skip the first peg of every row to form a nice edge. Bring the yarn to the inside of the loom, across the peg to be skipped, then back to the outside, ready to knit the next stitch *(Fig. 10a, page 17)*.

Row 1: Skip 1, K1, P2, K4, P2, K1, (P1, K1) across.

Row 2: Skip 1, K1, (P1, K1) 8 times, P3, K4, P2, K2.

Row 3: Skip 1, K1, P2, K4, P2, K1, (P1, K1) across.

Row 4: Skip 1, K1, (P1, K1) 8 times, P3, work Right Cross Cable, P2, K2.

Rows 5-278: Repeat Rows 1-4, 68 times; then repeat Rows 1 and 2 once **more**.

Work chain one bind off across.

Block piece to help make the cable stitches even **(see Blocking, page 26)**.

Fold Body in half matching cast on and bound off edges. Beginning at fold, weave seam for 9" (23 cm) **or** to desired length to form hood **(Fig. 16, page 26)**.

Weave in yarn ends.

GARTER WEDGES BABY BLANKET ....

INTERMEDIATE

Finished Size: 38" (96.5 cm) diameter

MATERIALS

Light Weight Yarn **LIGHT 3**
[5 ounces, 459 yards
(141 grams, 420 meters) per skein]:
  Color A (Blue) - 3 skeins
[4 ounces, 367 yards
(113 grams, 336 meters) per skein]:
  Color B (Print) - 3 skeins
62 Peg straight loom
Knitting loom tool
Crochet hook, size K (6.5 mm)
Yarn needle

Blanket is worked as flat knitting using two strands of yarn held together as one throughout.

GAUGE: In Garter Stitch,
       13 stitches and 32 rows = 4" (10 cm)

BODY

The cast on edge is equal to one half of the blanket diameter. After completing 8 wedges worked in short rows, the cast on and bound off edges will be joined.

With Color A, e-wrap cast on 62 pegs; drop yarn to the inside of the loom

When instructed to place marker, hold the working yarn at the inside of the loom, and place a short piece of yarn between peg just worked and next peg.

Row 1: With Color B and placing the beginning yarn end at the inside of the loom, leave the first peg unworked and knit across to last 4 pegs, place marker, K2, leave remaining 2 pegs unworked.

Short rows are formed by only working across some of the pegs. Reverse directions at the end of the written instructions for each row and wrap rows as indicated *(Figs. 15a & b, page 24)*.

Row 2: Purl across to last peg, K1.

When changing colors, drop yarn to the inside of the loom over the strand to be picked up *(Fig. 7d, page 13)*.

When instructed to **skip the first peg**, simply leave the first peg unworked. This method forms a nice edge along the outer edge of the blanket.

Row 3: With Color A, skip 1, knit across to marker, remove marker.

Row 4: P2, place marker, purl across to last peg, K1.

Row 5: With Color B, skip 1, knit across to marker, remove marker.

Row 6: P2, place marker, purl across to last peg, K1.

Rows 7-55: Repeat Rows 3-6, 12 times; then repeat Row 3 once **more**.

Row 56: Purl across to last peg, K1.

Row 57: Continuing with Color A, skip 1, K5, wrap next peg.

Row 58: Purl across to last peg, K1.

To knit a wrapped peg, knit the peg lifting both loops over the working yarn and off the peg.

Row 59: With Color B, skip 1, knit across to wrapped peg, knit wrapped peg and next peg, wrap next peg.

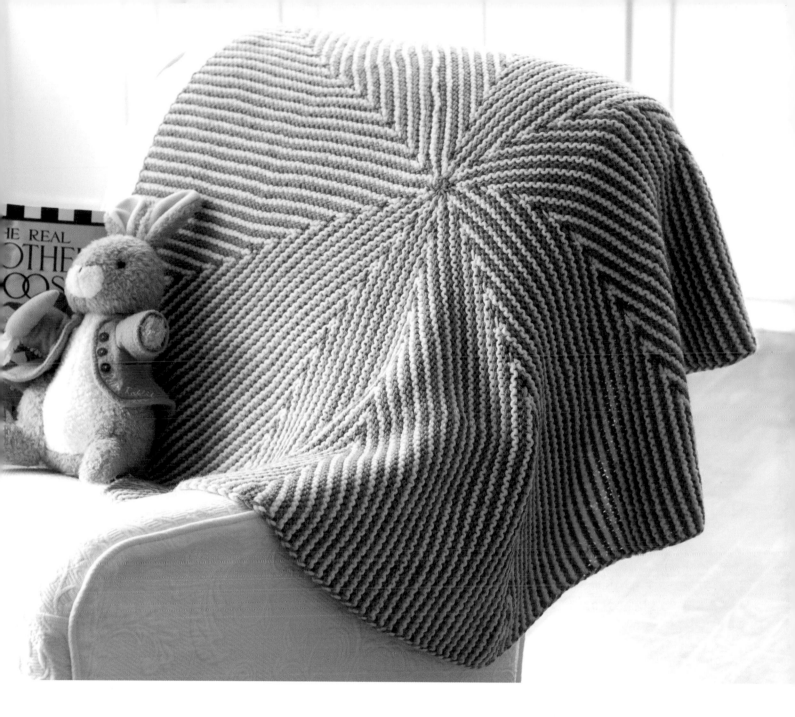

Row 60: Purl across to last peg, K1.

Row 61: With Color A, skip 1, knit across to wrapped peg, knit wrapped peg and next peg, wrap next peg

Row 62: Purl across to last peg, K1.

Rows 63-112: Repeat Rows 59-62, 12 times; then repeat Rows 59 and 60 once **more**.

Row 113: With Color A, skip 1, knit across to wrapped peg, knit wrapped peg and last peg.

Row 114: Purl across to last peg, K1.

Repeat Rows 1-114, 7 times.

Cut Color B.

Work chain one bind off across.

Sew cast on row to bind off row. Close any gap left at the center of the circle by weaving the yarn through the edge stitches; pull tightly and secure yarn.

Weave in yarn ends.

RIDGED LACE HAT ....

■■■▭ INTERMEDIATE

Finished Size: Fits most adults

MATERIALS
Bulky Weight Yarn **BULKY 5**
[3.5 ounces, 94 yards
(100 grams, 86 meters) per hank]:
  1 hank
48 Peg round loom
Knitting loom tool
Yarn needle

GAUGE: In pattern,
       12 stitches and 20 rows = 4" (10 cm)

STITCH GUIDE ....

YRP, RIGHT DECREASE
Move the loop from the next peg to the peg on
the right *(Fig. 13d, page 21)*. E-wrap the empty
peg clockwise to create the YRP, and bring the
yarn to the outside *(Fig. 14d, page 23)*. Knit
the next peg lifting the bottom 2 loops over
the working yarn and off the peg to create the
decrease *(Fig. 13e, page 21)*.

YRP, LEFT DECREASE
Skip the next peg and remove the loop from the
next peg using your fingers. Move the loop from
the skipped peg to the empty peg *(Fig. 14b,
page 22)*, then place the loop you are holding
on top of the loop you just moved. E-wrap the
empty peg clockwise to create the YRP, and
bring the yarn to the outside *(Fig. 14c, page 22)*.
Knit the next peg lifting the bottom 2 loops over
the working yarn and off the peg to create the
decrease.

PICOT HEM
Working as circular knitting and moving around the
loom counter-clockwise, e-wrap cast on 48 pegs.

Rnds 1-4: Knit around.

Rnd 5: (YRP, right decrease) around.

Rnds 6-9: Knit around.

To form hem, lift up the bottom edge toward the inside
of the loom and place the loops from the cast on row
over the pegs *(Fig. 21)*. There will be 2 loops on
each peg.
Lift the bottom loop on each peg over the top loop
and off the peg, securing the bottom edge and
leaving one loop on each peg.

Fig. 21

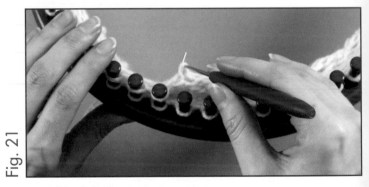

BODY

Rnd 1: Knit around.

Rnd 2: Purl around.

Rnd 3: Knit around.

Rnd 4: (YRP, right decrease) around.

Rnd 5: Knit around.

Rnd 6: Purl around.

Rnd 7: Knit around.

Rnd 8: (YRP, left decrease) around.

Rnds 9-35: Repeat Rnds 1-8, 3 times; then repeat Rnds 1-3 once **more**.

Cut yarn leaving a 18" (45.5 cm) length for sewing.

Work Gathered Removal to remove Hat from loom and to close top of Hat *(Figs. 3a & b, page 7)*.

Weave in yarn ends.

Block Hat to stretch lace stitches out *(see Blocking, page 26)*.

LACE WRAP ··························

Finished Size: 15" x 67" (38 cm x 170 cm)

MATERIALS

Medium Weight Yarn **(MEDIUM 4)**
[1.75 ounces, 109 yards
(50 grams, 100 meters) per skein]:
  7 skeins
62 Peg straight loom
Knitting loom tool
Crochet hook, size K (6.5 mm)
Yarn needle

GAUGE: In pattern,
        16 stitches and 20 rows = 4" (10 cm)

STITCH GUIDE ···························

LEFT DECREASE, YRP
Skip the next peg and move the loop from the next peg to the skipped peg. Knit the peg lifting the bottom 2 loops over the working yarn and off the peg to create the decrease **(Figs. 13a & b, page 20)**. E-wrap the empty peg clockwise to create the YRP **(Fig. 14a, page 22)**, and bring the yarn to the outside.

YRP, LEFT DECREASE
Move the loop from the next peg to the peg on the left. E-wrap the empty peg counter-clockwise to create the YRP, and bring the yarn to the outside. Knit the next peg lifting the bottom 2 loops over the working yarn and off the peg to create the decrease **(Fig. 14e, page 23)**.

LEFT E-WRAP DECREASE, YRP
Remove the loop from the next peg using your fingers. Move the loop from the next peg to the empty peg, then place the loop you are holding on top of the loop you just moved **(Fig. 14f, page 23)**. E-wrap knit the peg lifting the bottom 2 loops over the top loop and off the peg to create the decrease. E-wrap the empty peg counter-clockwise to create the YRP, and bring the yarn to the outside.

YRP, LEFT E-WRAP DECREASE
Skip the next peg and remove the loop from the next peg using your fingers. Move the loop from the skipped peg to the empty peg **(Fig. 14b, page 22)**, then place the loop you are holding on top of the loop you just moved. E-wrap the empty peg clockwise to create the YRP, and bring the yarn to the outside **(Fig. 14c, page 22)**. E-wrap knit the next peg lifting the bottom 2 loops over the top loop and off the peg to create the decrease.

WRAP
Working as flat knitting, chain cast on 60 pegs.

Skip the first peg of every row to form a nice edge. Bring the yarn to the inside of the loom across the first peg, then back to the outside, ready to knit the next stitch **(Fig. 10a, page 17)**.

Row 1: Skip 1, knit across.

Row 2: Skip 1, K7, left decrease, YRP, (K6, left decrease, YRP) across to last 2 pegs, K2.

Row 3: Skip 1, P2, (YRP, left decrease, P6) across to last peg, K1.

Row 4: Skip 1, K5, left decrease, YRP, (K6, left decrease, YRP) across to last 4 pegs, K4.

Row 5: Skip 1, P4, YRP, left decrease, (P6, YRP, left decrease) across to last 5 pegs, P4, K1.

Row 6: Skip 1, K3, (left decrease, YRP, K6) across.

Row 7: Skip 1, (P6, YRP, left decrease) across to last 3 pegs, P2, K1.

Row 8: Skip 1, K1, left decrease, YRP, (K6, left decrease, YRP) across to last 8 pegs, K8.

Row 9: Skip 1, P7, left e-wrap decrease, YRP, (P6, left e-wrap decrease, YRP) across to last 2 pegs, P1, K1.

Row 10: Skip 1, K2, YRP, left e-wrap decrease, (K6, YRP, left e-wrap decrease) across to last 7 pegs, K7.

Row 11: Skip 1, P5, left e-wrap decrease, YRP, (P6, left e-wrap decrease, YRP) across to last 4 pegs, P3, K1.

Row 12: Skip 1, K4, YRP, left e-wrap decrease, (K6, YRP, left e-wrap decrease) across to last 5 pegs, K5.

Row 13: Skip 1, P3, left e-wrap decrease, YRP, (P6, left e-wrap decrease, YRP) across to last 6 pegs, P5, K1.

Row 14: Skip 1, (K6, YRP, left e-wrap decrease) across to last 3 pegs, K3.

Row 15: Skip 1, P1, left e-wrap decrease, YRP, (P6, left e-wrap decrease, YRP) across to last 8 pegs, P7, K1.

Rows 16-337: Repeat Rows 2-15, 23 times.

Row 338: Skip 1, knit across.

Work chain one bind off across.

Weave in yarn ends.

Block Wrap *(see Blocking, page 26)*.

FELTED CANDY CANE STOCKING

Finished Size: approximately 5" wide x 18" high
(12.5 cm x 45.5 cm) after felting

MATERIALS
Medium Weight 100% Wool Yarn
[3.5 ounces, 223 yards
(100 grams, 205 meters) per skein]:
  Red - 1 skein
  White - 1 skein
48 Peg round loom
Knitting loom tool
Crochet hook, size K (6.5 mm)
Yarn needle

Gauge is not important in felted items, since there are so many variables in the felting process.

CUFF
With Red and working as circular knitting, chain cast on 48 pegs.

Rnd 1: Purl around.

Rnd 2: Knit around.

Repeat Rnds 1 and 2 until Cuff measures approximately 5" (12.5 cm) from cast on edge; drop yarn to the inside of the loom.

BODY
When instructed to **skip peg(s)**, bring the yarn to the inside of the loom across the peg(s) to be skipped, then back to the outside, ready to knit the next stitch *(Fig. 10a, page 17)*.

Rnd 1: With White and placing the beginning yarn end at the inside of the loom, K1, (skip 2, K2) around to last 3 pegs, skip 2, K1.

Rnd 2: K2, (skip 1, K3) around to last 2 pegs, skip 1, K1.

Rnd 3: With Red *(Fig. 7c, page 13)*, K1, skip 1, K2, (skip 2, K2) around.

Rnd 4: K1, (skip 1, K3) around to last 3 pegs, skip 1, K2.

Rnd 5: With White, K3, (skip 2, K2) around to last 5 pegs, skip 2, K3.

Rnd 6: K4, (skip 1, K3) around.

Rnd 7: With Red, K2, (skip 2, K2) around to last 2 pegs, skip 1, K1.

Rnd 8: K3, (skip 1, K3) around to last 5 pegs, skip 1, K4.

Rnds 9-88: Repeat Rnds 1-8, 10 times.

Cut White.

HEEL
Begin working in short rows, reversing directions at the end of each row and wrapping pegs as indicated *(Figs. 15a &b, page 24)*.

Row 1: With Red, K 12, wrap next peg.

Row 2: K 24, wrap next peg.

Rows 3-18: Knit across to within 1 peg of wrapped peg (peg with 2 loops on it), wrap next peg.

To knit a wrapped peg, knit the wrapped peg and lift both loops over the top loop and off the peg. When wrapping the same peg more than once, place the new wrap **above** the last one.

Rows 19-34: Knit across to wrapped peg, knit wrapped peg, wrap next peg.

Row 35: K 12.

FOOT
Begin working as circular knitting.

Rnds 1-48: Repeat Rnds 1-8 of Body, 6 times.

Cut White.

TOE
With Red, knit 10 rounds.

Cut Red leaving a 18" (45.5 cm) length for sewing

Work Gathered Removal to remove Stocking from loom and to close Toe *(Figs. 3a & b, page 7)*.

Weave in yarn ends.

FINISHING
Felt and shape Stocking *(see Felting, page 27)*.

Fold cuff over to desired length.

Attach ribbon or crocheted chain to inside of Cuff for hanger.

PANDA HAT ....

INTERMEDIATE

Finished Sizes:
Infant - 12½" (32 cm)
Child - 16½" (42 cm)

Size Note: Instructions are written for Infant's size with child's size in braces { }. Instructions will be easier to read if you circle all the numbers pertaining to your size. If only one number is given, it applies to both sizes.

MATERIALS

Light Weight Yarn
[5 ounces, 459 yards
(141 grams, 420 meters) per skein]:
  White - 1 skein
  Black - 50 yards (45.5 meters)
38{50} Peg straight loom
Knitting loom tool
Crochet hook, size K (6.5 mm)
Yarn needle
Attachable eyes - optional

CAUTION: If the hat is for an infant or any wearer that is at risk of choking on eyes, please use yarn for eyes.

Entire hat is worked holding two strands of yarn together as one throughout (pull one strand from center and one from the outside).

GAUGE: In pattern,
12 stitches and 12 rows = 4" (10 cm)

BODY
With White and working as circular knitting, begin with end peg and chain cast on all pegs.

Rnd 1: E-wrap knit around.

Rnd 2: Knit around.

Rnds 3-16: Repeat Rnds 1 and 2, 7 times.

NOSE
Begin working in short rows wrapping pegs as indicated *(Figs. 15a & b, page 24)* and reversing directions when instructed to turn.

Row 1: EWK 13{15}, wrap next peg; turn.

Row 2: EWK 2{4}, wrap next peg; turn.

To e-wrap knit a wrapped peg, e-wrap the wrapped peg and lift both loops over the top loop and off the peg.

Every third row ends back at the beginning. The yarn end indicates the beginning of the row. The next row is continued in the same direction.

Row 3: E-wrap knit across to beginning.

Row 4: K7, EWK 7{9}, wrap next peg; turn.

Row 5: EWK 4{6}, wrap next peg; turn.

Row 6: EWK 7{9}, knit across to beginning.

Row 7: EWK 15{17}, wrap next peg; turn.

Row 8: EWK 6{8}, wrap next peg; turn.

Row 9: E-wrap knit across to beginning.

Row 10: K7, EWK 9{11}, wrap next peg; turn.

Row 11: EWK 8{10}, wrap next peg; turn.

Row 12: EWK 9{11}, knit across to beginning.

Row 13: EWK 15{18}, wrap next peg; turn.

Row 14: EWK 6{10}, wrap next peg; turn.

Row 15: E-wrap knit across to beginning.

Row 16: K7, EWK 7{10}, wrap next peg; turn.

Row 17: EWK 4{8}, wrap next peg; turn.

Row 18: EWK 7{10}, knit across to beginning.

FOR CHILD'S SIZE ONLY
Row 19: EWK 16, wrap next peg; turn.

Row 20: EWK 6, wrap next peg; turn.

Row 21: E-wrap knit across to beginning.

Row 22: K7, EWK 8, wrap next peg; turn.

Row 23: EWK 4, wrap next peg; turn.

Row 24: EWK 8, knit across to beginning.

CROWN
Begin working as circular knitting.

Rnd 1: E-wrap knit around.

Rnd 2: Knit around.

Repeat Rnds 1 and 2, 2{3} times.

Cut yarn leaving an 18" (45.5 cm) length for sewing.

Work Gathered Method to remove Hat from loom and to close top of Hat (Figs. 3a & b, page 7).

Instructions continued on page 66.

MUZZLE

The nose is the area that was worked in short rows. In order to stabilize this area, thread yarn needle with a short length of a single strand of White yarn. Work a running stitch along wrapped stitches forming a "circle". Remove needle and slightly pull the running yarn to form the nose area; secure yarn.

DUPLICATE STITCH NOSE

Using 2 strands of Black, following chart and using photo as a guide for placement, work duplicate stitch for nose as follows:

Each knit stitch forms a V and you want to completely cover that V, so that the design appears to have been knit into the piece. Each shaded square on the chart below represents one e-wrap knit stitch that is to be covered by a Duplicate Stitch.
Thread a yarn needle with an 18" (45.5 cm) length of yarn. Beginning at the bottom of the design and with **right** side facing, bring the needle up from the wrong side at the base of the V, leaving an end to be woven in later (never tie knots). The needle should always go between the strands of yarn. Follow the right side of the V up and insert the needle from right to left under the legs of the V immediately above it, keeping the yarn on top of the stitch **(Fig. 22a)**, and draw through. Follow the left side of the V back down to the base and insert the needle back through the bottom of the same stitch where the first stitch began **(Fig. 22b)**; one duplicate stitch completed **(Fig. 22c)**. Continuing to follow chart, bring needle up through the next stitch. Repeat for each stitch, keeping tension even with tension of knit fabric to avoid puckering.

HALF CIRCLE (Make 6)

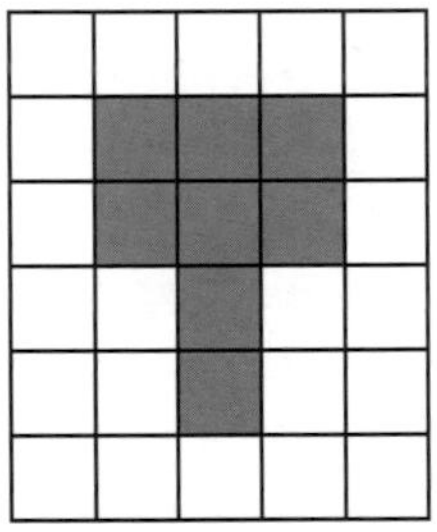

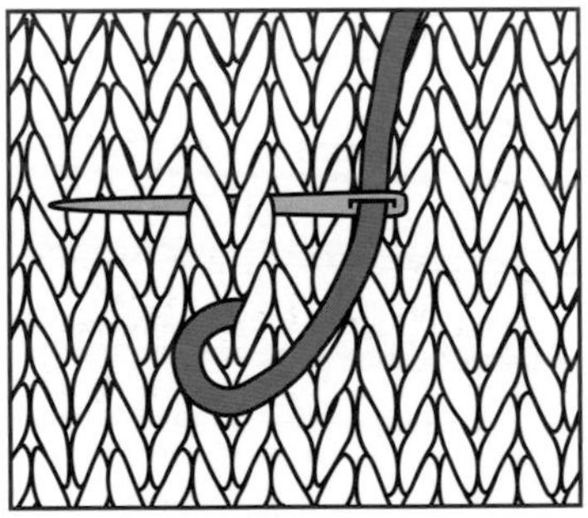

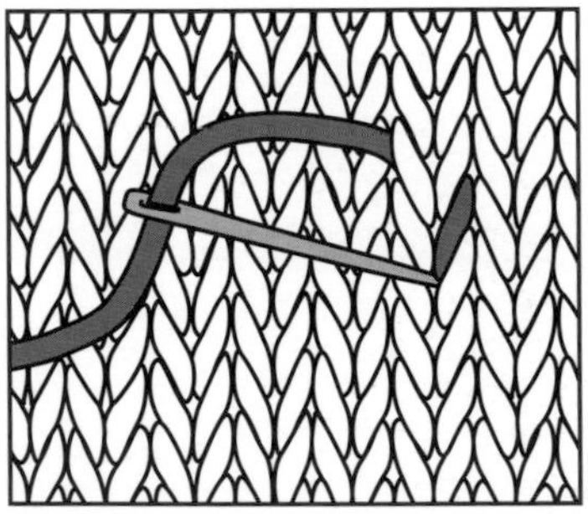

With Black, chain cast on 10 pegs.

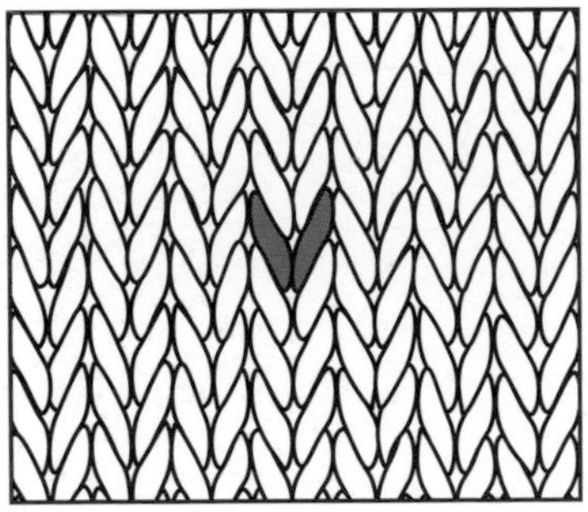

E-wrap knit 4 rows.

To work a gathered bind off, ★ Transfer the first loop to the next peg, lift the bottom loop over the top loop and off the peg; repeat from ★ until only one loop remains.

Cut yarn leaving a long end for sewing, and pull end through remaining loop.

Pin one Half Circle on each side of the nose for the eye patches, with bound off edge toward center. Sew in place.

Sew the **wrong** side of two Half Circles together for each ear. Using photo as a guide for placement, attach each ear to top of hat.

Attach eyes or use White to duplicate stitch the eyes over the black backgrounds.

Weave in yarn ends.

CHART

Fig. 22a

Fig. 22b

Fig. 22c

YARN INFORMATION ....

The items in this leaflet were made using a variety of yarns. Any brand of the specified weight of yarn may be used. It is best to refer to the yardage/meters when determining how many balls or skeins to purchase. Remember, to achieve the same look, it is the weight of the yarn that is important, not the brand of yarn.

For your convenience, listed below are the specific yarns used to create our photo models.

BEGINNER KNIT HAT
Red Heart® Bamboo Wool
#3920 Cayenne

NEXT-STEP E-WRAP KNIT HAT
Red Heart® Eco-Ways™ Bamboo Wool
#3525 Peacock

GARTER STITCH BRIM HAT
Red Heart® Eco-Ways™ Bamboo Wool
Color A (Teal) - #3525 Peacock
Color B (Gold) - #3265 Gold

SAMPLER AFGHAN
Red Heart® Eco-Ways™
Color A (Brown) - #3360 Mushroom
Color B (Teal) - #3518 Peacock
Color C (Lt Teal) - #3520 Aquarium

CORN ON THE COB HAT & SCARF SET
Lion Brand® Vanna's Choice®
Color A (Rust) - #133 Brick
Color B (Gold) - #130 Honey

HONEYCOMB HAT & SCARF SET
Premier™ Yarns, Deborah Norville
Serenity Chunky Weight
DN700-21 Pristine

FELTED BASKETWEAVE TOTE
Lion Brand® Fishermen's Wool
Color A (Brown) - #126 Nature's Brown
Color B (Ecru) - #098 Natural

HOODED VEST
Patons® Shetland Chunky
#03520 Russet

LATTICE PILLOW
Red Heart® Eco-Ways™
Color A (Brown) - #3360 Mushroom
Color B (Lt Teal) - #3520 Aquarium

BEJEWELED FINGERLESS GLOVES
Lion Brand® Vanna's Choice®
#140 Dusty Rose

ROBIN'S HOOD
Lion Brand® Wool-Ease® Thick & Quick®
#131 Grass

GARTER WEDGES BABY BLANKET
Lion Brand® Babysoft®
Color A (Blue) - #107 Bluebell
Color B (Print) - #293 Twinkle Print

RIDGED LACE HAT
Louet™ North America
Gems Chunky Weight
#05 Goldilocks

LACE WRAP
GGH Tara
#25 Fuchsia

FELTED CANDY CANE STOCKING
Patons® Classic Wool
Red - #00230 Bright Red
White - #00202 Aran

PANDA HAT
Lion Brand® Babysoft®
#100 White
#153 Black

INDEX

We have made every effort to ensure that these instructions are accurate and complete. We cannot, however, be responsible for human error, typographical mistakes, or variations in individual work.

PRODUCTION TEAM:
Instructional Editor - Cathy Hardy
Editorial Writer - Susan McManus Johnson
Graphic Artists - Jacob Casleton,
    Angela Ormsby Stark, and Janie Wright
Senior Graphic Artist - Lora Puls
Photo Stylist - Angela Alexander
Photographers - Jason Masters and Ken West